TOP 10
AMSTERDAM

FIONA DUNCAN & LEONIE GLASS

D0095555

EYEWITNESS TRAVEL

Left **De Hollandse Manege** Right **Magere Brug**

LONDON, NEW YORK,
MELBOURNE, MUNICH AND DELHI
www.dk.com

Produced by DP Services, London

Printed and bound in China
by Leo Paper Products Ltd

First American Edition, 2003
13 14 15 16 10 9 8 7 6 5 4 3 2 1

Published in the United States by DK Publishing,
375 Hudson Street, New York, New York 10014

**Reprinted with revisions 2005, 2007, 2009,
2011, 2013**

**Copyright 2003, 2013 © Dorling Kindersley
Limited, London**

ISSN 1479-344X
ISBN 978-0-75669-595-8

Within each Top 10 list in this book, no hierarchy
of quality or popularity is implied. All 10 are, in the
editor's opinion, of roughly equal merit.

Floors are referred to throughout in
accordance with Dutch usage; ie the "first floor"
is the floor above ground level.

MIX
Paper from
responsible sources
FSC™ C018179

Contents

Amsterdam's Top 10

AMSTERDAM'S TOP 10

TOP 10 Amsterdam Highlights

Amsterdam has an appeal that is absolutely unique. It's a vibrant place, a treasure-trove of extraordinary artistic riches, and the living embodiment of 900 years of history, during which it rose to become the centre of a huge global empire. After a period of decline, it matured into today's relaxed and tolerant modern metropolis. Elegant and serene, Amsterdam also has its seamy side, and this too is part of its character, as much as its famous network of canals. Whatever you are looking for, this small city packs a big punch.

Canals and Waterways **1**

Amsterdam's canals – in particular, the elegant ring of three 17th-century canals known as the Grachtengordel – are its defining feature *(see pp8–11)*.

2 Rijksmuseum

The country's largest national museum houses an unrivalled collection of 17th-century Dutch art, and much besides. Star exhibits include Vermeer's *Milkmaid (left)* and Rembrandt's *Night Watch (see pp12–15)*.

Van Gogh Museum **3**

The Van Gogh Museum houses simply the most comprehensive collection of the artist's work to be seen anywhere in the world – including some of his most famous paintings. The collection also includes works by other 19th-century artists *(see pp16–19)*.

4 Museum Ons' Lieve Heer op Solder

Things are not always what they seem, and that is certainly true of this gem of a 17th-century house in the Red Light District: tucked away on its upper floors is a rare example of a perfectly preserved hidden Catholic church. The rest of the museum is fascinating, too – the church interior has been restored and modernized. *(see pp20–21)*.

Map labels: Brouwersg..., Jordaan, Prinsengracht, Keizersgracht, Herengracht, 9, Bloemgracht, RAADHUISSTRAAT, ROZENGRACHT, Jordaan, KEIZERSGRACHT, SPUISTRAAT, Negen Straatjes, Singel, MARNIXSTRAAT, NASSAUKADE, Her..., LEIDSESTRAAT, Keizersgr..., LEIDSE PLEIN, Prinsengrach..., STADHOUDERSKADE, HOBBEMAST..., WETERINGSCHANS, Lijnbaansgracht, STADHOUDE..., VAN BAERLESTRAAT, P.C. HOOFTST..., 2, VAN PAULUS POTTER STR, 3, MUSEUM PLEIN, STADIONWEG..., HOBBEMAKADE

5 Begijnhof

A haven of peace, the Begijnhof was built as a refuge for the Beguines, a lay Catholic sisterhood. Amsterdam's oldest house is here *(see pp22–3)*.

6 Amsterdam Museum

Housed in the old city orphanage, this vibrant collection traces the history of Amsterdam from the 12th century *(see pp24–7)*.

7 Oude Kerk

This great Gothic basilica preserves a number of its treasures, despite being stripped of its paintings and statuary during the Iconoclasm *(see pp28–9)*.

Nieuwe Zijde
Oude Zijde
Oosterdok
Oudeschans
Wertheim Park
Artis Plantage
Amstel
Rembrandt Plein
Frederiks Plein

DAMRAK
ROKIN
WARMOESSTRAAT
GELDERSEKADE
GELDERSEKADE
PRINS HENDRIKKADE
PRINS HENDRIKKADE
IJTUNNEL
NIEUW MARKT
KLOVENIERSBURGWAL
KLOVENIERSBURGWAL
JODENBREESTRAAT
VALKENBURGERSTRAAT
MR VISSERPLEIN
MUIDERSTRAAT
WEESPERSTRAAT
PLANTAGE MIDDENLAAN
UTRECHTSESTRAAT
IZERSGRACHT
SARPHATISTRAAT

4 7
8

500 yards — 0 — metres 500

8 Museum Van Loon

Visitors to the Van Loon family residence on the Keizersgracht, lovingly restored in the style of the mid-18th century, have a rare opportunity to see behind the façade of a grand canal house – and to wander freely about it *(see pp30–31)*.

9 Anne Frank House

The hiding place of Anne Frank and her family, before they were discovered, arrested and sent to their deaths, is today a deeply moving museum *(see pp32–3)*.

10 Dam Square

Where it all started: Amsterdam's main square is on the site of the dam on the Amstel around which the city grew. Now it hosts concerts, events and all shades of city life *(see pp34–5)*.

⚡10 Canals and Waterways

With their delightful views, pretty bridges (1,703 in all), idiosyncratic gabled houses and relaxed waterside cafés, Amsterdam's 75 km (47 miles) of canals are full of interest and perfect for a leisurely stroll. They are a constant reminder that the Netherlands is the world's flattest country, half of which has been reclaimed from the sea with the aid of dykes, canals and huge tidal barriers. Before you start exploring Amsterdam's canals on foot, you should take a boat tour (see pp10 and 136) for a fascinating overview. In 2010 the 17th-century canal ring was added to the UNESCO World Heritage List.

Café Van Puffelen

🖧 Three perfect canalside cafés are Papeneiland, at Prinsengracht 2,Van Puffelen, where you can sit on a barge in summer *(see p102),* and De Sluyswacht *(see p80).*

🌀 If you are in the centre of Amsterdam, with no time to explore the city's canals, at least take a stroll to the Huis op de Drie Grachten, (House on Three Canals), step-gabled on all three of its canal-facing sides, at Oudezijds Voorburgwal 249.

Top 10 Canals and Waterways

1. Herengracht
2. Keizersgracht
3. Prinsengracht
4. Entrepotdok
5. Reguliersgracht
6. Amstel River
7. Brouwersgracht
8. Bloemgracht
9. Leidsegracht
10. Singel

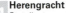

Herengracht
Stateliest canal of the Grachtengordel *(see p11),* the Herengracht is famous for its Golden Bend – a grand but rather lifeless stretch of mansions built for the richest merchants. A more beautiful stretch lies between Huidenstraat and Leidsestraat, best viewed from the east side.

Keizersgracht
The central canal of the Grachtengordel has fine stretches between Brouwersgracht and Raadhuisstraat, and again between Runstraat and Leidestraat.

Prinsengracht
The outermost canal of the Grachtengordel, designed for warehouses and artisans' housing, has a breezy, laid-back air. It is peppered with cafés, art galleries and houseboats. Cycle its 3 km (2 mile) length, or explore short stretches on foot.

Entrepotdok
An imposing stretch of former dockland has been restored to provide offices and apartments, with outdoor cafés overlooking colourful houseboats.

Reguliersgracht
Much loved for its pretty houses and hump-backed bridges, Reguliersgracht was cut in 1664. Look out for Nos 57, 59 and 63.

Amstel River
Until the construction of the Grachtengordel pushed it out of focus, the river Amstel was the city's *raison d'être*. It is still used by barges to transport goods to the city's port.

Brouwersgracht
The happy-go-lucky feel of the "brewers" canal makes a pleasant contrast to the sophisticated elegance of the Grachtengordel.

Bloemgracht
A charming canal crossed by cast-iron bridges, Bloemgracht is known locally as "the Herengracht of the Jordaan", because of its elaborately gabled houses.

Leidsegracht
This lovely – and exclusive – canal was cut in 1664, when it was the main barge route from Amsterdam to Leiden.

Singel
Once a fortified moat, the Singel is now home to Bloemenmarkt, the domed Ronde Lutherse Kerk and the soaring Neo-Gothic Krijtberg church.

How Amsterdam's Houses are Built

Each house is built on wooden piles sunk into the marshy, porous subsoil. It wasn't until the 17th century, when the piles could be sunk deep enough to reach the hard layer of sand that lies at 13 m (42 ft), that any real stability was achieved. Some reach even further, to a second layer of sand at 18 m (58 ft). If piles come into contact with air, they rot, so today, concrete is used instead of wood.

Left **Canal tour boat on the Oudeschans** Right **De Poezenboot**

Unexpected Sights on a Canal Tour

1 The Safest Vaults
The vaults of the Dutch National Bank are sunk some 15 m (48 ft) below ground level. In the event of an alarm, they have been designed to allow the waters of the Singelgracht to flood into them.

2 The Prison Bridge
The Torensluis – the widest bridge in Amsterdam – spans the Singel on the site of a 17th-century sluice gate. A lock-up jail was built into its foundations.

3 The Cat Boat
Hundreds of feline waifs and strays are given refuge in *De Poezenboot* (The Cat Boat), moored on the Singel *(above)*.

4 The Drunken Tsar
In 1716, Peter the Great got drunk at his friend Christoffel Brants' house at Keizersgracht 317, and kept the mayor waiting at a civic reception. That night, he stayed at the house of the Russian ambassador, Herengracht 527, where Napoleon also stayed in 1811.

5 The Narrowest House
Is Singel 7 the smallest house in Amsterdam? No, it's simply the back door of a wedge-shaped house, whatever your tour guide tells you.

6 Blue Angel
Cast your eye upwards to the beautiful Blue Angel statue perched on the former *Levensverzekering Maatschappij - Noord-Braband* building, at the corner of Singel and Haarlemmerstraat.

7 The Most Crooked Café
Teetering Café de Sluyswacht, built in 1695, makes an alarming sight as you glide by along the Oudeschans *(see p80)*.

8 The Wrapped-up House
Look carefully at Victoria Hotel, near the station, and you will see two tiny 17th-century houses embedded in the monumental 19th-century façade. A little old lady, so the story goes, refused to sell up, so the hotel had to wrap itself around them.

Peter the Great

9 The Floating Pagoda
The famous Sea Palace, Amsterdam's floating Chinese restaurant, makes an unusual sight and romantic dinner spot, with its twinkling lights and many windows.

10 The Tower of Tears
This medieval defensive tower has the saddest of names: Schreierstoren (Tower of Tears), where weeping women waved farewell to their seafaring men.

The Grachtengordel

Declared a UNESCO World Heritage Site in 2010, Amsterdam's magnificent semicircle of three canals – Prinsengracht, Keizersgracht and Herengracht – is the city's defining characteristic. Lined by elegant gabled houses, and connected by intimate cross-streets, it was devised in the early 17th century to cope with the rapid rise in population, and was built in two stages during the century. This costly Plan of Three Canals was purely aesthetic – the land along the banks was sold in single plots; the wealthy bought two together so that they could build larger houses.

Amsterdam had its unlikely beginnings some 400 years before, when a fishing settlement grew up on the marshy banks of the river Amstel. (It was dammed in 1222 – hence the name, a contraction of Amstelledamme.) As the town began to expand, canals were cut to drain more land and provide transport channels, and outer canals were fortified. A glance at a map clearly shows the limits of the medieval town, bounded by the curved Singel, with the Grachtengordel fanning out beyond.

Magere Brug

Built in 1672 and so narrow that it was named the Skinny Bridge, this much-loved double-leaf wooden drawbridge was rebuilt in 1969.

Plan of Amsterdam (1648) showing the Grachtengordel

For details of canal tours **See p136**

TOP 10 Rijksmuseum

The magnificent national museum of the Netherlands possesses nearly seven million works of art, only a fraction of which is on display. It was established by King Louis Napoleon in 1808 in the Royal Palace on the Dam, moving to its present location near the Vondelpark in 1885. The main building, designed by P J H Cuypers, underwent extensive renovation for 10 years, reopening in 2013. The museum posesses an unrivalled collection of Dutch art, with more than 8,000 pieces.

Façade of the Rijksmuseum

🍴 The Groot Café on the ground floor overlooking the Atrium is a great place to crowd watch while you rest your weary feet.

🕐 Be prepared: the museum has more than 8,000 items of Dutch art dating from the Middle Ages to the 20th century. With 80 rooms spread over four floors, don't expect to see everything in a single visit. The Philips Wing is currently being renovated. It will reopen in 2014.

• Museumstraat 1
• Map D5
• 020 674 7000
• www.rijksmuseum.nl
• Open 9am–6pm; closed Jan 1
• Admission €14 (under 19s free); garden free

Key

- Ground floor
- First floor
- Second floor

1 The Night Watch
The museum's most prized possession is *The Military Company of Captain Frans Banning Cocq* – otherwise known as *The Night Watch* (1642), given pride of place in a section of the Philips Wing.

2 The Jewish Bride
In creating one of the most tender double portraits ever painted (1667), Rembrandt depicted – in an unusually free style – an unknown couple in the guise of biblical characters Isaac and Rebecca.

3 The Kitchen Maid
The sense of realism in this painting by Vermeer (c.1658) is conveyed by his mastery of light, colour and perspective. Seen slightly from below against a bare wall, the simple, sturdy girl seems almost tangible – quiet and still, but for the milk flowing from her jug *(below)*.

4 Portrait of a Girl Dressed in Blue
This portrait by Johannes Verspronck (1641) is a wonderful example of the artist's signature polished style of painting. Smooth, almost invisible brush strokes contrast significantly with the rougher styles of contemporaries such as Frans Hals *(see p46)*.

Due to extensive renovation, the locations of the Top 10 works are unknown at the time of updating.

Top 10 Works

1. The Night Watch
2. The Jewish Bride
3. The Kitchen Maid
4. Portrait of a Girl Dressed in Blue
5. Temple Guard
6. Windmill on the Polder Wate
7. Our Lady of Sorrows
8. FK23 Bantam
9. The square man
10. Royal Marriage Coffers

Temple Guard
5 This depiction of temple guard Naraen Kongo (Ungyo) dates from between 1300 and 1400 and is made from wood with traces of polychromy *(right)*.

Our Lady of Sorrows
7 This unique Flemish terracotta bust (c.1500–1510) is a lifelike depiction of Mary in mourning; the Mater Dolorosa *(below)*.

The square man
9 *The square man* (1951) is typical of Karel Appel's work during his CoBrA years, defining the face of Dutch art in this period.

Royal Marriage Coffers
10 Created by the celebrated Parisian furniture maker, André-Charles Boulle (c.1688), these paired marriage coffers are a fine example of the artist's work, representing the Renaissance styles of tortoiseshell and gilded bronze.

Windmill on the Polder Wate
6 Paul Joseph Constantin Gabriel's balanced composition *(left)* is heavily influenced by Impressionist ideas, with its use of quick brushstrokes. It was acquired by the Rijksmuseum in 1889 and was considered modern for the time.

FK23 Bantam
8 Designed by Frits Kookhoven in 1917, this aeroplane is an icon of the Dutch contribution to aviation. Featuring a fuselage with wooden frames, wooden propeller and wicker pilot's chair.

Gallery Guide
The museum is split into eras with the Middle Ages, Renaissance, Special Collections and Asian Pavilion housed on the ground floor; 18th- and 19th-century art on the first floor; 17th-century Golden Age on the second floor; and 20th-century pieces on the third floor. There are four main entrances, all located within the Atrium. Two lead to the East wing, and two to the West. Due to the extensive renovation, items on display may be moved around the gallery.

For more on Dutch Artists See pp46–7

Left, Centre **Works by Edvard Munch and Gerard Ter Borch** Right **Seated Guanyin**

Rijksmuseum Features

1 The Building
The architect P J H Cuypers attracted strong criticism from the Protestant community, who took exception to the building's Neo-Gothic roofs and ornately decorated façade. King William III refused to set foot inside.

2 The Garden
A little-known, immaculate haven, it is studded with statues and architectural curiosities.

3 Atrium
The entrance and heart of the museum, the two courtyards of the Atrium – now restored to their original 1885 condition – are linked by an underground passageway.

4 Terazzo Floor
Covered in 1920 and hacked away in the late 20th century, Cuypers' original terrazzo floor has been restored to its former glory. Hundreds of thousands of small marble stones make up this floor, which is rich in symbolism.

5 Library
The library is only open to researchers of art history but, museum visitors can look through a large glass wall to view its impressive interior and book collection.

Museum Floorplan

6 Asian Pavilion
A quiet, meditative place, this is a wonderful retreat from the swarming masses. Elsewhere, Dutch art proliferates; the Asian Pavilion offers an insight into a different culture and time – that of Asia many ages ago.

7 Special Collection
The Special Collection ranges from amusing to bizarre: rooms full of boxes, animals, Meissen porcelain, miniature silver, an armoury, and even the hair of Jacoba of Bavaria, the 15th-century Countess of Holland and Zeeland.

8 The Golden Age
Renowned the world over for its 17th-century collection, visitors flock to the Rijksmuseum to see paintings by Dutch Masters such as Rembrandt, Vermeer, Jan Steen and Frans Hals.

9 Modern Art
Two loft-like spaces on the third floor house art from the 20th century: one 1900–1950; the other 1950–2000.

10 Great Hall
The Great Hall on the second floor has been entirely reconstructed to resemble how it looked in Cuypers' day, with elaborate and beautiful late 19th-century decoration.

 Locations of collections/exhibits are unknown at the time of update

Top 10 Events in Rembrandt's Life

1. Born in Leiden (1606)
2. Studies with Pieter Lastman (1624)
3. Receives first important commission and marries Saskia van Uylenburgh (1634)
4. Reputation grows; buys large house in Amsterdam (1639) – now the Museum het Rembrandthuis
5. Titus, his only child to survive into adulthood, is born (1641)
6. Saskia dies; *The Night Watch* completed (1642)
7. Hendrickje Stoffels moves in (1649)
8. Applies for bankruptcy (1656)
9. Titus and Hendrickje acquire the rights to his work
10. Death of Titus (1668); in October of the following year, Rembrandt dies

Rembrandt and *The Night Watch*

Popular belief holds Rembrandt's greatest painting, The Night Watch (1642), responsible for his change in fortune from rich man to pauper. In fact, it was more a case of poor financial management than of public dissatisfaction with the artist, although it's very likely that the militiamen who commissioned the portrait would have been dismayed at the result. The Night Watch *differs radically from other contemporary portraits of companies of civic guards, in which they are depicted seated, serious and soberly dressed (see p26). Rembrandt, by contrast, shows a tumultuous scene – the captain issuing orders to his lieutenant, the men taking up arms ready to march. This huge painting was originally even larger, but it was drastically cut down in 1715, when it was moved to the town hall, and the other pieces were lost. In 1975 it was slashed, but repaired.*

Self-Portrait as St Paul

Rembrandt's series of self-portraits, painted throughout his life, provide an extraordinary insight into his character.

The Military Company of Captain Frans Banning Cocq – better known as The Night Watch

Van Gogh Museum

The most comprehensive collection in the world of Van Gogh's work was amassed by his art dealer brother Theo, and is housed in this museum. It includes more than 200 of his paintings, over 500 drawings and hundreds of letters, as well as his Japanese prints and works by contemporaries – though not all are on permanent display. Gerrit Rietveld's airy building, opened in 1973, sets off the paintings to perfection. The display follows Van Gogh's development from the murky peasant scenes of the early 1880s to the anguished final works. Due to renovation some works may be shown at the nearby Hermitage Museum.

Van Gogh Museum façade

🍴 The museum has a useful self-service café, situated on the ground floor.

⏰ To avoid the crowds, arrive at opening time or buy tickets at the museum's website *(see below)*. Stick to the chronological order of the display.

- Paulus Potterstraat 7
- Map C6
- 020 570 5200
- www.vangogh museum.com
- Open 10am–6pm daily, 10am–10pm Fri
- Admission: adults €14 (under 12s free)
- Audio tours €2.50–4; group tours by appointment

Sunflowers
This vibrant painting (1889) was intended to be one of a series of still lifes to fill the "Yellow House" at Arles. Van Gogh chose sunflowers because he was expecting Paul Gauguin, and knew his friend liked them. The predominant yellows and oranges contrast with strokes of brilliant mauve and red.

The Potato Eaters
The culmination of his years in Nuenen, this was Van Gogh's first major composition (1885). He wanted to portray the peasants realistically, not glamorize them, but the painting was not the critical success he had hoped for.

The Bridge in the Rain
This work, painted in 1887, illustrates Van Gogh's interest in Japanese art, in particular Utagawa Hiroshige. However, Van Gogh used far brighter colours and greater contrasts.

Top 10 Paintings

Key

- Basement
- Ground floor
- First floor
- Second floor
- Third floor

A Pair of Shoes

Van Gogh gives character to a pair of worn boots in one of the first paintings after his move to Paris (1886). The dark palette harks back to his Nuenen work.

Self-Portrait as an Artist

The last and most accomplished in a series of self-portraits painted in 1887, shortly before he left Paris, reveals Van Gogh's distinctive interpretation of Pointillism. He chose himself as subject since he could seldom afford models.

Fishing Boats on the Beach at Les Saintes-Maries-de-la-Mer

A trip to the sea in 1888 produced these colourful, stylized boats. Look close and you will see grains of sand, blown on to the canvas and fixed there forever as the paint dried.

The Reaper

While undergoing treatment in Saint-Rémy, Van Gogh found solace painting people who worked the land. He painted three versions of The Reaper (1889).

Wheatfield with Crows

One of the panoramic landscapes that Van Gogh painted in 1890, during the last days of his life, this famous picture with its dead-end track and menacing, crow-filled sky, perhaps reveals his tortured state of mind.

Vincent's Bedroom in Arles

The mastery of this painting (1888) lies in the simplicity of the subject and the subtly alternating blocks of colour. Van Gogh was so happy with the result that he made two copies (see p19).

Almond Blossom

Van Gogh made this picture of white almond blossom against a blue sky for his new nephew, born in January 1890 and named after him.

Museum Guide

Van Gogh's paintings are displayed by date and place of execution on the first floor of the main building. Works by contemporaries are split between ground and third floor. Exhibitions of drawings and graphic art are staged on the second floor, which also has a study area, where drawings and documents too fragile to be displayed can be viewed. The Exhibition Wing has three floors, devoted to temporary exhibitions.

For more Amsterdam museums See pp40–41

Left **Exhausted Maenads** Centre **Amsterdam cityscape by Monet** Right **Gauguin self-portrait**

TOP 10 Van Gogh Museum: Other Artists

1 View of Prins Hendrikkade and the Kromme Waal in Amsterdam
Monet painted this cityscape in winter 1874 from a boat on the IJ river.

2 Young Peasant Girl with a Hoe
Jules Breton was an idol of Van Gogh. In rural scenes like this one (1882), he places an idealized figure in a realistic setting.

3 Exhausted Maenads after the Dance
In this Lawrence Alma-Tadema painting of 1874, three devotees (maenads) of the wine god Bacchus have fallen asleep.

4 Portrait of Guus Preitinger, the Artist's Wife
The vivid use of colour in Kees van Dongen's portrait of his wife (1911) is characteristic of Fauvism.

5 Young Woman at a Table, "Poudre de Riz"
This early painting by Toulouse-Lautrec (1887), who became a friend of Van Gogh, is probably of his mistress, Suzanne Valadon.

6 Portrait of Bernard's Grandmother
Van Gogh swapped one of his self-portraits for this painting (1887) by Emile Bernard.

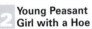

Museum Floorplan

7 Saint Geneviève as a Child in Prayer
An oil study (1876) by Puvis de Chavannes for the huge murals he painted on the theme of St Geneviève's childhood at the Panthéon in Paris.

8 Self-Portrait with a Portrait of Bernard, "Les Misérables"
In his powerful self-portrait (1888), Gauguin identified himself with the hero of *Les Misérables*, Jean Valjean.

9 "Grand Paysan"
Jules Dalou shared Van Gogh's preoccupation with peasants, whom he saw as heroic labourers. He devised this life-size sculpture in 1889.

10 Two Women Embracing
Van Gogh's influence on the Dutch artist Jan Sluijters is obvious in the brushwork and colour of this painting of 1906.

Portrait of Bernard's Grandmother

The Life of Vincent van Gogh

Born on 30 March 1853 in Zundert, Vincent van Gogh was the eldest son of a pastor and his wife. Aged 16, he joined his uncle's business Goupil & Co., art dealers. Seven years later, displaying increasingly erratic behaviour, he was dismissed. After a couple of false starts as teacher and evangelist, in 1880 he decided to be a painter. From 1883 to 1885, he lived with his parents in Nuenen, but in 1886 he went to Paris to study in Fernand Cormon's studio. He lived with his brother Theo, met renowned artists and changed his style. In 1888, he moved to Arles where he dreamed of establishing an artists' colony with Paul Gauguin. Soon after Gauguin arrived, the friends had a fierce argument, and during a psychotic attack, Van Gogh cut off a piece of his own left ear lobe. He enrolled as a voluntary patient in a clinic in Saint-Rémy in 1889. The following year he left for the rural village Auvers-sur-Oise, where his state of mind deteriorated and he shot himself in the chest on 27 July 1890. He died, with Theo at his bedside, two days later.

Vincent Van Gogh

Vincent's Bedroom in Arles

Museum Ons' Lieve Heer op Solder

Contrasting sharply with its surroundings in the shabbiest corner of the Red Light District, this 17th-century house has a surprise in store. Concealed in its upper floors is a church, Ons' Lieve Heer op Solder (Our Lord in the Attic). Restored in 2011, it's a rare, perfectly preserved example of the many clandestine churches built after the Alteration (see facing page). Local Catholics worshipped here from 1663 to 1887, when nearby St Nicolaaskerk was built. Its little-changed interiors transport you back in time to the Dutch Golden Age.

Façade with spout gable

For refreshment, head to the Nieuwmarkt, where In de Waag is an excellent café-restaurant.

Take one of the free plans and follow the suggested tour of the museum. If you are confused at first, don't worry – all the rooms are clearly marked and you won't miss anything.

• Oudezijds Voorburgwal 40
• Map P2
• 020 624 6604
• www.opsolder.nl
• Open 10am–5pm Mon–Sat, 1–5pm Sun, public hols. Closed 1 Jan, 30 Apr
• Admission: €7; concessions: €5; under 19: €1

Top 10 Features

1. The Building
2. Canal Room
3. The Sael
4. The Priest's Room
5. The Hidden Church
6. The Folding Pulpit
7. The Maria Chapel and Peat Room
8. The Confessional
9. The Rear Houses
10. The Kitchen

1 The Building

The spout-gabled canal house was built in 1661 for Jan Hartman, a Catholic merchant. He combined its attic with the attics of two smaller houses behind to create the hidden church, which was extended in c.1735.

2 Canal Room

This 17th-century living room *(above)* overlooks the canal to the front, and is where residents spent most of their time during the day. It is decorated with furnishings from the era, including a replica stove.

3 The Sael

Adhering to strict rules of proportion and symmetry, the family's formal parlour *(sael)* is a superb example of the Dutch Classical style fashionable in the 17th century *(below)*. It contrasts with the simpler Canal Room, which would not have been used to receive guests.

For more on Amsterdam's churches See pp42–3

The Chaplain's Room

Formerly the servants' quarters, the Chaplain's Room is in a corner on a bend in the stairs. It's a tiny, enclosed bedroom with a box bed, simply furnished as it would have been for the priest of the hidden church, who lived in the house.

Key

■	Ground floor
■	First floor
■	Second floor
■	Third floor
■	Fourth floor
■	Fifth floor

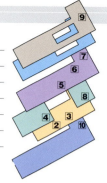

The Hidden Church

At the top of the stairs, the hidden church (*schuilkerk*) proves a charming and highly unusual sight (*left*). In c.1735 it was remodelled in Baroque style, with the addition of two tiers of galleries, suspended from the roof by cast-iron rods, to provide extra seating.

The Folding Pulpit

With space-saving in mind, the ingenious pulpit was designed to fold away under the left column of the altar when not in use. The altar painting is *The Baptism of Christ* by Jacob de Wit (1695–1754).

The Maria Chapel

This chapel comprises a small altar dedicated to the Virgin Mary. The statue is one of the few original objects belonging to the 17th-century church.

The Confessional

In 1739, this living room in the middle of the three houses became the church's confessional. One of the two wooden confessional boxes still remains (*right*).

The Rear Houses

The rear houses were gradually taken over by the church, but there are still signs of their original use as family rooms.

The Kitchen

Once part of the sacristan's secret living quarters, the charming 17th-century kitchen (*left*) has Delft wall tiles, an open hearth, stone sink and black-and-white floor.

The Alteration

The revolt of the (Calvinist) Northern Netherlands against the (Catholic) Spanish Habsburgs began in 1568, but Amsterdam did not decide where its loyalties lay until 1578, when the city joined William of Orange in a peaceful revolution known as the Alteration. Calvinists seized power and Amsterdam became the Protestant capital of an infant Dutch republic. Catholics were no longer allowed to worship in public, but Dutch tolerance ensured that they were able to continue in private.

➡ *For more on the Dutch Golden Age* **See p27**

Begijnhof

Away from the bustle of the city, this bewitching sanctuary of elegant houses around a tranquil green was founded in 1346 for the members of a lay Catholic sisterhood, the Beguines, the last of whom died in 1971. Although none of the original buildings survive – nor the early design in which the courtyard was surrounded by water – there is a fascinating example of a 15th-century wooden house, a lovely church of the same period, and an appealing hidden chapel. Visitors are asked to respect the privacy of the current residents.

The elegant houses of the Begijnhof

Café Luxembourg and traditional Café Hoppe are just round the corner in Spui (at Nos 18 and 24 respectively).

Services are held in Dutch (daily) and French (Sundays) in the Roman Catholic Begijnhof Chapel. Services in English are held in the Protestant Engelse Kerk (Sundays).

Enjoy a lunchtime concert at the Engelse Kerk.

Pick up an information booklet from Het Houten Huis.

• Spui (entrance on Gedempte Begijnensloot)
• Map M4
• 020 623 3565
• www.begijnhof amsterdam.nl
• Open 9am–5pm daily; Begijnhof Chapel open 1–6:30pm Mon, 9am–6:30pm Tue–Fri, 9am–6pm Sat & Sun
• Free

Top 10 Features

1. Engelse Kerk
2. Begijnhof Chapel
3. Het Houten Huis
4. Courtyard with Wall Plaques
5. Mother Superior's House
6. 17th- and 18th-Century Houses
7. Statue of a Beguine
8. The Beguine in the Gutter
9. Wall Plaque on No. 19
10. Spui Entrance

Engelse Kerk

Before the Alteration *(see p21)*, the Beguines worshipped in this pretty 15th-century church *(below)*. Confiscated in 1578, it was let in 1607 to a group of English and Scottish Presbyterians, who renamed it.

Begijnhof Chapel

The city's first clandestine chapel was created in 1665, when the Beguines converted two ordinary houses into a little church *(see pp20–21)*. The Miracle of Amsterdam *(see p38)* is commemorated here.

Het Houten Huis

No. 34, Het Houten Huis, is the oldest house in Amsterdam *(below)*, and one of only two wood-fronted houses in the city. It predates the 1521 ban on the construction of wooden houses, introduced to reduce the risk of fire.

4 Courtyard with Wall Plaques

Set into the wall of the courtyard behind Het Houten Huis is a remarkable collection of wall plaques salvaged from demolished houses. In keeping with the religious nature of the Beguines, each one tells a Biblical story.

5 Mother Superior's House

The grandest house, No. 26, belonged to the Mother Superior *(above)*. In the 20th century, the last of the Beguines lived together here.

Plan of the Begijnhof

6 17th- and 18th-Century Houses

After several devastating fires, most of the existing houses were built in the 17th and 18th centuries. They are typically tall and narrow, with large sash windows and spout or neck gables. They were the property of the sisterhood, so if a Beguine left or died, outsiders could not claim her house. Today they provide homes for 100 or so single women.

7 Statue of a Beguine

The statue shows a Beguine dressed in her traditional *falie* (headdress) and long garment of undyed cloth.

8 The Beguine in the Gutter

To make amends for her family's conversion to Protestantism, Cornelia Arents requested in her will not to be buried in the church, but in the gutter outside. Her coffin was left inside the church on 2 May 1654, but the following day it had miraculously moved outside, where she was eventually buried. A plaque marks the spot.

9 Wall Plaque on No. 19

This handsome plaque *(above)* illustrates the return from Egypt to Israel of Jesus, Mary and Joseph after the death of Herod.

10 Spui Entrance

Members of the public use the arched entrance from Gedempte Begijnensloot, but be sure to peep discreetly into the pretty vaulted and tiled passageway leading to Spui.

The Welfare System

Charity lies at the heart of Amsterdam's long tradition of caring for the poor and needy, which goes back to the Middle Ages and continues to the present day. In the 14th century, primary responsibility for social welfare passed from the church to the city authorities. They distributed food to the poor, and set up institutions to care for orphans, the sick and the insane. In the 17th century, a number of wealthy merchants funded almshouses – *hofjes* – providing subsidized mass housing. Some of these *hofjes* are still used for their original purpose today.

 For more on hofjes **See p92**

Amsterdam Museum

The Amsterdam Museum houses the city's most fascinating collection of artifacts, archaeological finds, clothes, jewellery, maps, paintings and sculptures. Originally a convent, in 1580 it became the city orphanage. Handsome extensions were added by Hendrick and Pieter de Keyser before Jacob van Campen's magnificent rebuilding of 1634. The orphans moved out in 1960, and in 1975 the museum moved in. Stunning exhibits and interactive displays chart Amsterdam's growth and metamorphosis over the centuries.

Kalverstraat entrance, 1581

🔵 **Café Mokum is inside Joost Bilhamer's Kalverstraat entrance.**

🔵 **Start your sight-seeing here; it will help you understand the city when you begin to explore.**

The 45-minute Amsterdam DNA is a must *(see p26).*

Don't miss the delightful façade stones set into the wall of the museum in St Luciënsteeg.

• *Kalverstraat 92; Sint Luciensteeg 27*
• *Map M4*
• *020 523 1822*
• *www.amsterdam museum.nl*
• *Open 10am–5pm Mon–Sun; Closed 1 Jan, 30 Apr, 25 Dec*
• *Admission: adults €10; children 6–18 €5 (under 6s free)*

Top 10 Works

1. Bird's-eye View of Amsterdam
2. The Gouden Leeuw on the IJ by Amsterdam
3. Terrestrial and Celestial Globes
4. White Car
5. Dam Square
6. Turbo Shell
7. Orphan Girls going to Church
8. Dr F M Wibaut (bronze head)
9. The Anatomy Lesson of Dr Jan Deijman
10. Model of the Oosterdok

1 Bird's-eye View of Amsterdam
Cornelis Anthonisz's 1538 map of Amsterdam (the oldest extant) includes the Dam, Oude Kerk and Nieuwe Kerk.

2 The Gouden Leeuw on the IJ by Amsterdam
Willem van de Velde's painting (1686) shows the Gouden Leeuw with a view of Amsterdam across the IJ.

3 Terrestrial and Celestial Globes

A pair of costly globes lent prestige to any self-respecting 17th-century intellectual. Joan Willemsz Blaeu must have made this unique pair after 1644 because they show the Australian coast, just discovered by Abel Tasman (see p39).

4 White Car

Take a virtual drive in Luud Schimmelpennink's Witkar (White Car). The idea was conceived around 1970 and it was one of the first car share projects in the world. The electric cars are unlocked with a magnetic key.

5 Dam Square

George Hendrik Breitner based his cityscapes on photographs; despite its Impressionist style, this famous painting (1895–98) still has a photographic quality.

6 Turbo Shell

This exquisite mother-of-pearl *turbo marmoratus* is covered in tiny engraved animals. It dates from around 1650 and was probably brought from the Orient by the Dutch East India Company (VOC).

Key

- ■ Ground floor
- ■ First floor
- ■ Second floor

7 Orphan Girls going to Church

Nicolaas van der Waaij's charming painting of around 1895 hangs in the anteroom to the Regents' Chamber.

8 Dr F M Wibaut

This powerful bronze head was made in 1934 by Tjipke Visser, favourite sculptor of the Social Democratic Workers' Party (SDAP). The subject was Floor Wibaut, SDAP Councillor for housing in the 1920s, who dedicated himself to building new apartments for the working class.

9 The Anatomy Lesson of Dr Jan Deijman

In Rembrandt's original, eight surgeons watched Dr Deijman dissect a corpse. Fire destroyed most of the painting in 1723, but the frontal perspective of the remaining group is still quite remarkable.

10 Model of the Oosterdok

This wonderful model of the Oosterdok Lock dates from 1831, the year work started on the lock itself. It was part of a larger project to counteract a build-up of silt, which barred large ships from the harbour.

Museum Guide

Amsterdam DNA – the story of the city from its beginnings as a trading port to the modern day – is housed on the first floor. "Het Kleine Weeshuis" (The Little Orphanage) is on the ground floor, portraying the museum's former life. The permanent exhibition is displayed on all three floors, with a temporary exhibition space on the ground floor. The Civic Guards Gallery is located by the entrance. There is wheelchair accessibility at the St Luciënsteeg museum entrance.

For more Amsterdam museums **See pp40–41**

Left **Dam Square with the New Town Hall under Construction** Right **Civic Guard**

🔟 Amsterdam Museum Rooms

1 Civic Guards Gallery
The gallery houses one of the Netherlands' largest paintings: Matthieu van Bree's *The Entry of Napoleon in Amsterdam* (1815).

2 Regents' Chamber
The orphanage governors met in this 17th-century room, sympathetically restored in Old Holland style.

Museum Floorplan

3 Room 2: Walking through the City
Aptly named, this room includes a superb collection of 14th- and 15th-century leather shoes, well preserved after centuries in mud.

4 Room 4: Turbulent Times
Displays from the late 16th century include the Civic Guard's Italian-made armour, and silver that escaped melting down for "crisis coins" in 1578.

5 Room 6: The Dam
The bustling heart of the city was a popular subject in 17th-century paintings like Lingelbach's *Dam Square with the New Town Hall under Construction*.

6 Amsterdam DNA
This 3-D exhibition takes visitors on a 45-minute historical tour of Amsterdam, telling the multifaceted story of the City in seven chronological chapters.

7 Room 12: The 18th Century
The 18th century saw the decline of Amsterdam and, ultimately, the Republic's defeat by the French. A highlight is the museum's collection of 18th-century miniature silver toys.

8 Room 15: 19th-century Cabinet
There was a 19th-century trend for rich industrialists to collect art. These important collections helped establish the public ownership of art.

9 Room 22: Amsterdam 1940–1945
A room devoted to memorabilia of the German occupation.

10 Room 24: Café 't Mandje
A meticulous reconstruction of leather-clad motorbiker Bet van Beeren's famous café on Zeedijk – the first where homosexuals could be open.

Café 't Mandje

Top 10 Highlights of the Golden Age

1. *The Night Watch* by Rembrandt (1642, Rijksmuseum) *(see p15)*
2. The Grachtengordel, designed by Hendrick Staets (begun in 1613) *(see p11)*
3. Museum Amstelkring (1663) *(see pp20–21)*
4. Westerkerk by Hendrick de Keyser (1631) *(see p91)*
5. Huis met de Hoofden, sometimes attributed to Pieter de Keyser (1622) *(see p91)*
6. Claes Claeszhofje (1616)
7. Silver Marriage Cup by Gerrit Valck (1634) *(right)*
8. Café Hoppe (c.1670) *(see p50)*
9. Delftware (second half 17th century)
10. Burgerzaal (Paleis op de Dam) Koninklijk Paleis *(see pp34 & 39)*

The Golden Age

The economic boom of the 17th century laid the foundations for the flowering of the arts in Amsterdam. Plans were laid to surround the city with a triple ring of canals lined with fine houses, a project which required the work of many architects. The most powerful city in the Dutch Republic recognized the importance of the arts, and rewarded its artists well – and with the supremacy of the Protestants came the freedom to paint secular subjects. To show their wealth and status, rich patrons commissioned portraits of themselves and their families. The artists' best clients, however, were the municipal bodies such as the guilds, who commissioned group portraits, as well as decorative pieces of silver and glass. Painters began to focus their energies on a single area of painting – whether historical, portraiture, interiors, genre, still lives, urban scenes, landscapes or seascapes – and this specialization greatly enhanced the quality of their workmanship.

Silver Marriage Cup
The hinged bowl above the woman's head forms one cup, her full skirt a second. Once the wedding was in full swing, bride and groom would down both together.

Dutch Battle Ships by Ludolf Backhuysen

Amsterdam's Top 10

Oude Kerk

The city's oldest monument and first parish church stands on the site of an early 13th-century wooden chapel that was destroyed by fire. Rebuilt as a small stone hall church in the 14th century, over the years it expanded into a mighty Gothic basilica, now in the heart of the Red Light District (see p77). The interior is stark, stripped of its Catholic treasures during the Iconoclasm of 1566, but it boasts some exquisite stained glass, rare ceiling paintings and a world-famous organ. It is dedicated to St Nicholas, patron saint of the city.

Exterior of the Oude Kerk

🍴 For food and people-watching, head for Nieuwmarkt; In de Waag (Nieuwmarkt 4) is recommended.

🕐 Go to the Dutch Reformed Church service at 11am on Sundays, one of the Spring or Summer concerts, or the World Press Photo exhibition (late April to early June).

Don't miss the votive ships hanging from the choir ceiling.

• Oudekerksplein South Entrance
• Map P2
• 020 625 8284
• www.oudekerk.nl
• Open 11am–5pm Mon–Sat, 1–5pm Sun. Closed 1 Jan, 25 Dec, 30 Apr
• Admission €5; concessions €4 (separate charge for exhibitions)
• Guided tours by appointment; Tower Apr–Sep: noon–4pm Sat–Sun; Oct–Mar: by appointment (phone 020 689 2565)

Top 10 Features

1. Great Organ
2. Maria Kapel
3. Ceiling
4. Saskia's Grave
5. Red Door into the Old Sacristy
6. Decorated Pillars
7. Misericords
8. Spire
9. Stained Glass of the Burgemeesters
10. Little Organ

1 Great Organ
With its eight pairs of bellows, magnificent oak-encased pipework, marbled wood statues and gilded carving, the great organ is a glorious sight *(right)*. Built by Christian Vater in 1724 and renovated by Johann Caspar Müller 14 years later, it is known as the Vater-Müller organ.

2 Maria Kapel
The most stunning stained glass is in the three windows of the Lady Chapel. All date from the 16th century; two show scenes from the Virgin's life, above the customary picture of the family who donated the window.

3 Ceiling
The massive wooden vaulted ceiling is claimed to be the largest in Western Europe, but it was only during restoration work in 1955 that the beautiful 15th-century paintings were revealed.

4 Saskia's Grave
Among the great and the good buried here is Saskia van Uylenburgh, Rembrandt's first wife, who died in 1642. Her grave is number 29K in the Weitkopers Kapel.

 Share your travel recommendations on traveldk.com

Red Door into the Old Sacristy

5 Rembrandt passed through this door to announce his marriage. "Marry in haste, repent at leisure" is inscribed above it.

Plan of the Oude Kerk

Decorated Pillars

6 Relics of the period before 1578, these pillars once supported niches for statues of the Apostles destroyed in the Iconoclasm, and were painted to look like brocade, since the real thing was too expensive, and unsuited to the humid atmosphere.

Misericords

7 The 15th-century misericords helped choristers take the weight off their feet *(left)*. They are decorated with charming carvings illustrating traditional Dutch proverbs.

Spire

8 From the graceful late-Gothic spire, built by Joost Bilhamer in 1565, there are splendid views over the Oude Zijde. The tower contains a 47-bell carillon, a 17th-century addition which rings out every Saturday afternoon.

Stained Glass of the Burgemeesters

9 The colourful stained glass windows flanking the chancel depict the arms of the city burgomasters from 1578 to 1807 *(left)*. One was designed by De Angeli in 1758; the other by Pieter Jansz in 1654.

Little Organ

10 Attractively painted shutters form the original casing (1658) – however, the pipework was replaced in 1965. Tuned as it would have been before 1700, early music can now be part of the repertoire.

The Iconoclasm of 1566

In the 1566 Iconoclasm, or *Beeldenstorm* – precursor to the Alteration of 1578 *(see p21)* when the city became Protestant – the Calvinists looted Catholic churches and destroyed their treasures, among them the Oude Kerk's pictures, altars and statues. Only the ceiling paintings and stained glass were spared, as they were out of reach. The Calvinists also disapproved of the beggars and pedlars who gathered in the church, and threw them out, ending its role as a city meeting place.

For more Amsterdam churches **See pp42–3**

⭐10 Museum Van Loon

Step back into the 18th century at this delightful canal house on Keizersgracht, which has been the property of the prestigious Van Loon family (co-founders of the Dutch East India Company, later bankers and royal courtiers) since 1884. In 1973 the family, who still reside here, opened it to the public, having painstakingly restored it to its appearance in the 1750s, when it was owned by Dr Abraham van Hagen and his heiress wife Catharina Trip. It is beautifully furnished with Van Loon family possessions throughout.

Façade of the Museum Van Loon

🍴 There is no café; head for nearby Nieuwe Spiegelstraat or Utrechtsestraat for a good choice.

👪 Serene and elegant, the Museum Van Loon makes a perfect visit for adults, but is not so well suited to young children.

- *Keizersgracht 672*
- *Map E5*
- *020 624 5255*
- *www.museum vanloon.nl*
- *Open 11am–5pm Wed–Mon*
- *Admission €8; concessions €6*
- *Guided tours on request*

Top 10 Features

1. The Building
2. The Staircase
3. The Family Portraits
4. The Wedding Portrait
5. The Garden
6. The Dining Service
7. The Gold Coin Collection
8. The Painted Room
9. The Romantic Double Portrait
10. The Kitchen

1 The Building
In 1672, Jeremias van Raey built two large houses on Keizersgracht. One he occupied himself, the other – No. 672, now the Museum Van Loon – he rented to Rembrandt's most famous pupil, Ferdinand Bol.

2 The Staircase
The balustrade was installed by Dr Van Hagen, who had his and his wife's names incorporated into the ornate brass work. When the canals ceased to freeze over regularly, the 18th-century sledge in the hall found a new use as a plant stand.

3 The Family Portraits
Portraits of the Van Loon family are displayed throughout the house.

4 The Wedding Portrait
Jan Molenaer's first major commission in Amsterdam portrays the whole family. It's a second marriage: the bride holds her stepson's hand in an act of acceptance, while the fallen chair symbolizes the groom's deceased brother.

5 The Garden

Laid out according to a plan of the property of 1700, the peaceful garden ends in the false Neo-Classical façade of the coach house *(below)*. Inside, displays include original Van Loon carriages, liveries and special exhibitions.

Key

- ■ Ground floor
- ■ First floor
- ■ Second floor

6 The Dining Service

Rare 18th-century Dutch porcelain and 19th-century Limoges ware grace the dining room.

7 The Gold Coin Collection

Over the centuries, five Van Loon couples have celebrated their golden wedding; each had gold coins specially minted.

8 The Painted Room

Painted wallpapers such as these, featuring ruins, Classical buildings and human figures, were very popular in the 1700s.

9 The Romantic Double Portrait

Painted by J F A Tischbein in 1791, this intimate, relaxed portrait of these Van Loon ancestors is typical of the Age of Enlightenment, conveying love and happiness as well as duty.

Museum Guide

Visitors are welcomed as guests in a private house and encouraged to wander around freely. They are allowed to walk on the carpets and nothing is roped off. Temporary exhibitions of modern art and sculpture are often on display in both the house and garden.

10 The Kitchen

Cosy and inviting, the basement kitchen has been restored to look as it did in a photograph of 1900.

Anne Frank House

This deeply moving museum tells a tragic story. When in 1942 the Germans began to round up Jews in Amsterdam, the Frank and Van Pels families went into hiding. For 25 months, they hid in a secret annexe in the Anne Frank Huis. In August 1944, they were betrayed and deported. Only Otto survived. The diary of his daughter, Anne, who died in Bergen-Belsen concentration camp in March 1945 at the age of 15, has made her one of the most inspiring figures of the 20th century. The ever-popular museum attracts thousands of visitors each year.

Façade of Prinsengracht 263

There is a pleasant, airy café, with a great view of the Westerkerk.

Book on-line to avoid the long queues.

Take care around the house as the stairs are steep and narrow.

The visit is a moving experience, so plan something contemplative afterwards: climb the Westerkerk spire, or walk to the Western Islands.

- Prinsengracht 263 (entrance at 267)
- Map L2
- 020 556 7105
- www.annefrank.org
- Open mid-Sep–mid-Mar: 9am–7pm daily (until 9pm Sat); Jul–Aug: 10am–10pm daily; mid-Mar–mid-Sep: 9am–9pm daily (until 10pm Sat). Closed Yom Kippur
- Admission adults €9; children 10–17 €4.50
- No disabled access

Top 10 Features

1. The Warehouse
2. The Offices
3. The Moveable Bookcase
4. The Secret Annexe
5. Anne's Room
6. Peter's Room
7. The Front Attic
8. The Diary Room
9. Otto Frank Exhibit
10. The Exhibition Room

The Warehouse

Otto Frank ran a business making pectin for jam, and spice and herb mixtures. The annexe in which the families hid was over his warehouse, so they had to keep quiet for fear that the warehouse workers would hear them.

The Offices

Visitors continue upstairs to the offices of Otto Frank and the staff who helped to hide him and his family, along with Otto's business partner, Hermann Van Pels, and his wife and son. In Anne's diary, the Van Pels became the Van Daans.

The Moveable Bookcase

To camouflage the entrance to the annexe, one of the helpers made a swinging bookcase. As Anne wrote, "no one could ever suspect that there could be so many rooms hidden behind..."

The Secret Annexe

The claustrophobic rooms in which the eight lived have been left unfurnished, as they were when the Germans cleared their possessions after their arrest. On one wall, pencil marks record the growth of Anne and her sister Margot.

Anne's Room

5 After a while, Margot moved in with her parents, and Anne had to share her room with a new member of the group, a dentist called Fritz Pfeffer – in Anne's estimation, "a very nice man". Anne's film-star pin-ups are still up on the wall.

Key to floorplan

- ■ Ground floor
- ■ First floor
- ■ Second floor
- ■ Third floor
- ■ Attic

8, **9** and **10** in separate building

Peter's Room

6 The small refuge of Peter Van Pels was actually the landing on the way up to the attic. Anne often spent time here talking with Peter.

The Front Attic

7 In a moving display, the fate of each member of the group unfolds. Anne and Margot died a month before Bergen-Belsen was liberated.

Otto Frank Exhibit

9 An interview with Otto Frank from 1967 and documents from his personal collection are on show here. A notebook containing entries made during Otto's return from Auschwitz is particularly poignant.

The Diary Room

8 As well as the now famous red-checked diary, which she kept every day, Anne wrote short stories and ideas for novels. As time went on, she began to edit her original diary with a book called *The Secret Annexe* in mind.

The Exhibition Room

10 In the multimedia exhibition space, visitors can participate in a video reconstruction on issues relating to the eight people in hiding.

Anne Frank's Diary

On the day the family were taken away, Miep Gies found Anne's diary. With the words "here is your daughter Anne's legacy to you", she handed it to Otto Frank on his return from Auschwitz. He prepared a transcript, and the diary was published to great acclaim in the Netherlands in 1947, and in Britain and the United States in 1952. It has since been published in more than 70 languages. Over 1 million people visit the museum each year.

 For more Jewish sights in Amsterdam **See pp48–9**

Dam Square

The very heart of Amsterdam, Dam Square – or "the Dam", as the locals call it – marks the site of the original 13th-century dam on the Amstel river (see p9). An architectural parade spanning six centuries includes the glorious Nieuwe Kerk and the Koninklijke Paleis. By the 17th century, with the town hall here and the Exchange nearby, the Dam had become the focus of Amsterdam's political and commercial life. The passage of years may have eroded some of its grandeur – but certainly none of its colour or its vitality.

A horse and trap near the Nationaal Monument

There are cafés in De Bijenkorf and the Nieuwe Kerk – the latter with a terrace overlooking the Dam.

Go to one of the concerts or exhibitions held at the Nieuwe Kerk.

• Map M3, N3
• Koninklijk Paleis: www.paleisamsterdam. nl. 020 620 4060. Admission: adults €7.50; children 5–18 €3.75; seniors/students €6.50, under 5s free
• Nieuwe Kerk: during exhibitions: 10am–5pm daily. 020 626 8168. www.nieuwekerk.nl. Admission charge
• Madame Tussauds Amsterdam: Peek & Cloppenburg Building. 020 522 1010. www. madametussauds.nl. Open 10am–5:30pm daily. Closed 30 April. Admission: adults €21; children 5–15 €17; under 5s free

Top 10 Sights

1. Koninklijk Paleis
2. Nieuwe Kerk
3. Nationaal Monument
4. Madame Tussauds Amsterdam
5. Damrak
6. De Bijenkorf
7. Rokin
8. Kalverstraat
9. Grand Hotel Krasnapolsky
10. Street Performances and Events

Koninklijk Paleis
Built as the town hall, Jacob van Campen's unsmiling Classical edifice symbolizes the civic power of 17th-century Amsterdam *(above)*. It is still used for state occasions *(see p39)*.

Nieuwe Kerk
Now a venue for exhibitions, the Nieuwe Kerk has hosted royal events since 1814. Treasures include a Jacob van Campen organ case and an elaborately carved pulpit by Albert Vinckenbrinck *(see p42)*.

Nationaal Monument
This 22 m (70 ft) obelisk commemorates the Dutch killed in World War II *(above & centre)*. Embedded in the wall behind are urns containing soil from the Dutch provinces and colonies.

4 Madame Tussauds Amsterdam

Displays at this outpost of the London waxworks range from the fascinating to the bizarre. Special effects, including animatronics, bring to life scenes from Holland's past.

5 Damrak

Damrak was once the medieval city's busiest canal, with ships sailing up to be unloaded at the Dam. In 1672 the canal was filled in, and Damrak developed into the hectic shopping street it is today.

Plan of Dam Square

6 De Bijenkorf

Amsterdam's best-known department store has a vast perfumery, designer fashion boutiques and much more.

7 Rokin

The Rokin had its heyday in the 19th century, when its broad sweep was a promenade for the well-to-do.

8 Kalverstraat

Music shops jostle for space with tacky clothes stores at the Dam end of this pedestrian shopping street.

9 Grand Hotel Krasnapolsky

Adolf Wilhelm Krasnapolsky, an emigré Polish tailor with ambition, rented the down-at-heel Nieuwe Poolsche Koffiehuis in the 1870s, swiftly transforming it into a fashionable hotel (below).

10 Street Performances and Events

Busking, mime, funfairs, book fairs, exhibitions, concerts – such things have gone on in the Dam since J Cabalt introduced his puppet show in 1900.

Inside the Koninklijk Paleis

The ponderous exterior belies the magnificent interior – especially the dramatic Burgerzaal (Citizen's Hall). See fine sculptures by Artus Quellien and Rombout Verhulst, ceilings and friezes by Rembrandt's pupils, and Empire furniture of Louis Napoleon. The Vierschaar (Tribunal) is a macabre room, still intact, where judges once pronounced the death sentence.

For more Amsterdam churches See pp42–3

Left **The Arrival of Napoleon at Dam Square** Right **German wartime propaganda poster**

Moments in Amsterdam's History

1 **c.1125: First Settlers**
Fishermen settled at the mouth of the Amstel river, building huts on man-made mounds called *terps* for flood protection. With the growth of the new settlement came feudal conflict between the self-made Counts of Holland and Lords van Amstel.

2 **1275: Freedom from Tolls**
In the earliest document to refer to Amsterdam, Count Floris V of Holland granted its citizens exemption from tolls when transporting their goods by river across his territory at The Hague.

3 **1345: Miracle of Amsterdam**
At a house in Kalverstraat, a priest gave a dying man the last sacraments. He was unable to keep down the communion wafer, so it was thrown on the fire. Next morning, the wafer was found intact among the embers. News of the miracle spread, and Amsterdam soon became a place of pilgrimage.

Miracle of Amsterdam

4 **1566 and 1578: Iconoclasm and Alteration**
As Protestantism swept northern Europe, Dutch Calvinists rebelled against their intolerant Spanish Catholic ruler, Philip II. In the *Beeldenstorm* or Iconoclasm, the Calvinists stormed the Catholic churches and destroyed their religious artifacts. The city finally became Protestant, in a peaceful revolution known as the *Alteratie* or Alteration (see p21).

5 **1609: Plans for the Grachtengordel**
The dawn of the Golden Age, when the arts flourished in Amsterdam (see p27), saw ambitious plans for a triple canal ring around the city (see p11). Herengracht, Keizersgracht and Prinsengracht were built in two stages, starting in 1613 and 1663.

6 **1634–37: Tulipmania**
The Dutch passion for tulips dates from the late 16th century, when the first bulbs were imported from Asia. In 1634, the tulip was quoted on the Stock Exchange, and speculation began. Fortunes were made overnight as the craze led to spectacular price increases; the inevitable crash caused scores of bankruptcies.

7 **1806: Kingdom of the Netherlands Established**
After the formation of the Batavian Republic in 1795, rule was shared between the invading French and the Dutch Patriots. In 1806, Napoleon Bonaparte took over the Republic, created the Kingdom of the Netherlands and installed his brother, Louis Napoleon, as head of state.

 Previous pages **Pairs of wooden clogs in a basket**

8 1940–45: German Occupation

Despite Dutch neutrality, Germany invaded Holland in May 1940. With the deportation of Jews to concentration camps from 1942 onwards, the Dutch Resistance became active and underground newspapers thrived. Canadian troops liberated Amsterdam on 5 May 1945.

9 Mid-1960s: Provo Demonstrations

The radical Provo movement took off in the 1960s, fuelled by antagonism to the city's transport and housing policies. Street demonstrations turned into full-scale rioting on 10 March 1966, the day of Princess Beatrix's wedding to German aristocrat Claus von Amsberg. The Provos won seats on the city council, but their popularity was short-lived.

10 2002: Wedding of the Crown Prince

On 2 February 2002, Crown Prince Willem-Alexander married Máxima Zorreguieta in the Nieuwe Kerk, followed by a reception in the Koninklijk Paleis. The couple have three daughters, Princesses Catharina-Amalia, Alexia and Ariane born in 2003, 2005 and 2007 respectively.

Wedding of the Crown Prince

Top 10 Historic Characters

1 William of Orange
"William the Silent" (1533–84) led the Protestant rebellion against Philip II. He was assassinated.

2 Willem Barentsz
This explorer (1550–97) failed to discover the north-east passage but left behind invaluable maps.

3 Frederik Hendrik
An effective politician, William of Orange's youngest son (1584–1647) became *Stadhouder* in 1625.

4 Pieter Stuyvesant
Stuyvesant (1592–1672) was Governor of the colony of Nieuw Amsterdam, later to be New York, from 1646–64.

5 Abel Tasman
In search of trade routes to South America, Tasman (1603–c.1659) discovered Tasmania and New Zealand.

6 Michiel de Ruyter
This revered Dutch admiral (1607–76) set fire to the English fleet in the Medway in 1667.

7 Jan de Witt
A leading politician in the Anglo-Dutch Wars (1625–72), he was killed by a mob.

8 William III
William (1650–1702) was *Stadhouder* from 1672 until his promotion to King of England in 1688.

9 Louis Napoleon
Brother of Napoleon I, Louis (1778–1846) was King of the Netherlands between 1806 and 1810.

10 Johan Thorbecke
Liberal Prime Minister Johan Rudolf Thorbecke (1798–1872) was architect of the 1848 Constitution.

Left **Rijksmuseum** Right **Het Scheepvaartmuseum**

Museums

Rijksmuseum
1 The world's greatest collection of 17th-century Dutch art, together with pieces from the Middle Ages to the 20th century, are housed in this great art museum *(see pp12–15)*.

Van Gogh Museum
2 The permanent home for hundreds of works by this troubled artist also displays work by his contemporaries *(see pp16–19)*.

Amsterdam Museum
3 First a convent, then the city orphanage, now a wonderful museum charting the history of Amsterdam and, in particular, its meteoric rise during the Golden Age *(see pp24–7)*.

Amsterdam Museum

Museum Ons' Lieve Heer op Solder
4 The 17th-century domestic interiors would be fascinating in themselves, but the astonishing thing about this historic canal house is the secret Catholic church hidden on its upper floors *(see pp20–1)*.

Stedelijk Museum

Stedelijk Museum
5 After an extensive renovation project the Stedelijk Museum reopened in 2012. A new wing designed by Benthem Crouwel Architekten has created more space for the museum's unique collection. The Stedelijk now contains 1100 sq m (11,840 sq ft) of underground exhibition space, a sculpture hall and the futurist "bathtub" for modern cutting-edge exhibitions. A gift shop and a café overlook the Museumplein *(see p115)*.

Anne Frank House
6 This world-famous yet movingly simple museum is dedicated to the young diarist who hid here from the Nazis with her family *(see pp32–3)*.

Museum Van Loon
7 Another canal-house-turned-museum, the Van Loon recreates high-society life in the 18th century *(see pp30–31)*.

Share your recommendations on traveldk.com

8 Museum Willet-Holthuysen

Like the Museum Van Loon, the Willet-Holthuysen affords a rare glimpse inside a grand canal house – and into the lives of the wealthy merchants who lived there. Built in 1685, the interior is decorated in 18th-century style. A mild sense of melancholy pervades the building *(see p107)*.

Museum Het Rembrandthuis

9 Het Scheepvaart Museum

Holding the largest collection of boats in the world, and crammed with fascinating objects, the Nederlands Scheepvaart became a museum in 1973, when the Dutch Navy vacated the building. Solid and four-square, Daniel Stalpaert's imposing classical-style arsenal was built for the Admiralty in 1656 during the Golden Age of Dutch maritime history. Interactive exhibits and children's activities have made the museum a much more user-friendly experience following four years of extensive renovation *(see p123)*.

10 Museum Het Rembrandthuis

Completely restored to look as it did in Rembrandt's day, this handsome red-shuttered house was the artist's home during his years of prosperity (1639–58). Entering the rooms is a little like stepping into a painting: there are typical Dutch interiors with black-and-white tiled floors, traditional box beds, and paintings by Rembrandt's contemporaries. Perhaps the two most fascinating sights here are the recreation of his studio, and his magical etchings, of which there is a permanent exhibition that changes regularly. Many show Rembrandt's compassion for the common people, beggars and street musicians. A video about the restoration work is shown in the basement *(see p77)*.

Left **Noorderkerk** Right **De Krijtberg**

Churches

Oude Kerk
1 The oldest and greatest of Amsterdam's churches *(see pp28–9)*.

Nieuwe Kerk
2 The second parish church in Amsterdam was built after the congregation outgrew the Oude Kerk. Burnt down in 1645, its oldest part is the choir, dating from around 1400 *(see pp34, 83)*.

Westerkerk
3 After the Alteration of 1578 *(see p21)*, the first Dutch Protestant churches to be built were the Zuiderkerk, the Noorderkerk and the Westerkerk – all designed by Hendrick de Keyser. The Westerkerk has the city's tallest tower, topped by the gaily painted imperial crown of Maximilian of Austria *(see p91)*.

Zuiderkerk

Zuiderkerk
4 The splendid spire, with its columns, clocks, pinnacles and onion dome, was much admired by Sir Christopher Wren, and is still a prominent city landmark, with great views over the city from the tower. The Zuiderkerk ceased to function as a church in 1929 *(see p81)*.

Noorderkerk
5 Hendrick de Keyser's last church, begun a year before he died in 1621 (its completion was supervised by his son Pieter), is quite different in style. Built for the poor of the Jordaan, it is an austere brick building with only the shortest of spires. Designed on a Greek Cross plan, it has a central pulpit and four hipped roofs.
◎ *Noordermarkt 44–48 • Map D2 • Open 11am– 1pm Mon, Thu, Sat (also open for regular afternoon concerts and 11am–3pm Wed, noon–5:30pm Sun Apr–Oct) • Free*

Engelse Kerk
6 In the middle of the Begijnhof, the pretty English Reformed Church got its name from the English (and Scottish) Presbyterians who worshipped there after it was requisitioned in 1578. There has been a church on this site since the end of the 14th century *(see pp22)*.

Väter-Müller organ, Oude Kerk

7 De Krijtberg

Like many Catholic churches in Amsterdam, De Krijtberg (meaning Chalk Mountain) is known by its nickname rather than its official name, Franciscus Xaveriuskerk (after St Francis Xavier, a founding Jesuit monk); designed in 1884 by Alfred Tepe, it replaced a clandestine Jesuit chapel *(see p21)*. It's an impressive building, with an elegant, twin-steepled Neo-Gothic façade and an ornate interior that stands in marked contrast to the austerity of the city's Protestant churches.

◈ *Singel 448 • Map M5 • Open 1:30–5pm Tue–Thu, Sun and 30 mins before services; 12:30pm & 5:45pm Mon–Fri; 5:15pm Sat; 9:30am, 11am, 12:30pm & 5:15pm Sun • Free*

8 Mozes en Aäronkerk

Here, the nickname comes from two gablestones depicting Moses and Aäron on the house fronts that hid a clandestine church within. It was replaced in 1841 by the present Neo-Classical building, its towers inspired by St Sulpice in Paris.

◈ *Waterlooplein 205 • Map Q5*

9 St Nicolaaskerk

Dedicated to the patron saint of seafarers, the church was commissioned by the congregation of *Ons' Lieve Heer op Solder (see pp20–21)*. A C Bleys, the architect, came up with a Neo-Baroque building.

◈ *Prins Hendrikkade 76 • Map Q1 • Open noon–3pm Mon & Sat; 11am–4pm Tue–Fri; mass 12:30pm Mon–Sat; 10:30am, 1pm (Spanish) Sun (12:30pm Fri Spanish also) • Free*

St Nicolaas Kerk

10 Waalse Kerk

This church – founded in 1409 – is all that is left of the convent of St Paul. Its name means Walloon Church, a reference to the Low Countries (now Belgium), from where Huguenots fled the Catholic terror. In 1586 they were given use of the Waalse Kerk so that they could continue their worship in French. It has a historic organ dating from 1680, renovated in 1734 by master organ builder Christian Müller. The church is a popular concert venue. ◈ *Oudezijds Achterburgwal 159 • Map P4*

Left **Paleis van Justitie** Right **Eerste Hollandsche Verzekeringsbank**

🔟 Historic Buildings

1 Schreierstoren
The Schreierstoren (Tower of Tears) is one of Amsterdam's oldest buildings *(see p10)* – a surviving fragment of the medieval city wall. ◈ *Prins Hendrikkade 94–5 • Map Q2*

2 In't Aepjen
One of two remaining wood-fronted houses in Amsterdam *(see p22)*, In't Aepjen was built in 1550 as a sailors' hostel, and is now a bar. The name means "In the monkeys": when sailors couldn't pay, they would barter – sometimes with pet monkeys *(see p80)*.

3 Oost-Indisch Huis
Seen from the courtyard, the impressive red-brick façade, with its ornate entrance and stone-dressed windows, was the height of corporate fashion. Headquarters

of the once mighty Dutch East India Company (VOC), it was built in 1605, probably by Hendrick de Keyser, and is now part of Amsterdam University. The 17th-century meeting room of the VOC lords has been restored. ◈ *Oude Hoogstraat 24 (entrance Kloveniersburgwal 48) • Map P4 • 9am–9pm daily*

De Gooyer Windmill

4 De Gooyer Windmill
If you are lucky, you might see the vast, streamlined sails of this 18th-century corn mill creak into motion. Built in 1725, the whole octagonal structure was painstakingly moved to its present site in 1814. ◈ *Funenkade 5 • Map H4*

5 Pintohuis
Named after the Portuguese merchant Isaac de Pinto, who paid an exorbitant 30,000 guilders for it in 1651, the building boasts an Italianate façade and ceiling paintings by Jacob de Wit. A branch of the public library is housed here. ◈ *Sint Antoniesbreestraat 69 • Map P4*

6 Trippenhuis
Justus Vingboons' grandiose façade with false middle windows (1662) concealed the two separate homes of the powerful Trip brothers – arms dealers, hence the pair of chimneys resembling cannons. ◈ *Kloveniersburgwal 29 • Map P4*

Schreierstoren

Scheepvaarthuis

West-Indisch Huis

7 The city of New York was conceived in the Dutch West India Company building, and Pieter Stuyvesant's statue still surveys the courtyard *(see p39)*. Built in 1615, its classical proportions belie its origins as a meat market. ✆ *Haarlemmerstraat 75, (entrance: Herenmarkt 99) • Map D2*

Paleis van Justitie

8 This sober, monumental building in Empire style is a conversion of the Almoners' Orphanage by city architect Jan de Greef. ✆ *Prinsengracht 434–6 • Map K6*

Eerste Hollandsche Verzekeringsbank

9 Gerrit van Arkel's eye-catching 1905 building is a fine example of *Nieuwe Kunst*, the Dutch version of Art Nouveau. Built for an insurance company, it houses lawyers' offices and PR companies. ✆ *Keizersgracht 174–6 • Map L2*

Scheepvaarthuis

10 Designed as shipping company offices by van der Mey, de Klerk and Kramer, this fanciful building (1916) is smothered in nautical whimsy – mariners, monsters, and mermaids. It is now a luxury hotel. ✆ *Prins Hendrikkade 108 • Map Q2*

Top 10 Architectural Features

1 Triangular Gable
This simple triangular-shaped gable can be seen on Het Houten Huis *(see p22)*.

2 Bell Gable
Fashionable in the late 17th and 18th centuries, bell-shaped gables can be flamboyant (Prinsengracht 126) or unadorned (Leliegracht 57).

3 Neck Gable
Made popular by Philips Vingboons, this gable has a raised centrepiece; Oude Turfmarkt 145 is an example.

4 Spout Gable
This plain triangular gable topped by a spout was used for warehouses, like those at Entrepotdok *(see p9)*.

5 Step Gable
Common from 1600 to 1665, this gable has steps on both sides: Huis op de drie Grachten has three *(see p8)*.

6 Wall Plaque
Before numbering was introduced, houses were identified by plaques *(see p23)*.

7 Claw Piece
Sculptures – frequently of dolphins – were made to fill the right angles of gables, as in Oudezijds Voorburgwal 119.

8 Mask
This type of Renaissance decoration depicts a human or animal face, and can be seen at Oudezijds Voorburgwal 57.

9 Cornices
From 1690, gables fell out of vogue and decorative top mouldings came in: examples line the Herengracht.

10 Pediment Carvings
Carvings often decorate the triangular or rounded form above doorways: see the Felix Meritis Building *(see p100)*.

Left *Allegory of Painting* by Vermeer Right *Wheatfield with Crows* by Van Gogh

TOP 10 Dutch Artists

1 Jan van Scorel

After prolonged stays in Germany, Venice and Rome, where he studied the works of Giorgione, Michelangelo and Raphael, Jan Van Scorel (1495–1562) returned to Utrecht in 1524. He introduced the techniques of the Renaissance to the Northern Netherlands; his portraits fuse Italian solidity of form with Netherlandish delicacy.

2 Rembrandt van Rijn

The greatest artist of the Dutch Golden Age *(see p15)*.

3 Frans Hals

Much loved for his technique of capturing character and fleeting expression in his sitters, Frans Hals (1580–1666) brought a new realism to portraiture in the 17th century. His fine group portraits of civic guards are displayed in the Frans Hals Museum in Haarlem *(see p72)*.

4 Johannes Vermeer

Relatively little is known about the life of this sublime Delft artist (1632–75), who inherited his father's art-dealing business and painted purely for pleasure. He gained some recognition in Holland during his lifetime, but his importance was not established until the late 19th century, and rests on less than 40 known works – mainly domestic interiors with figures – that are extraordinary in their handling of space, light and colour. He was married with 11 children. On his death, his wife was declared bankrupt, and his baker kept two of his paintings against unpaid bills.

Self Portrait as a Young Man by Rembrandt

5 Jan Steen

A prolific painter of the genre (everyday) scenes so popular in the Dutch 17th century, Jan Steen (1625–79) was an innkeeper as well as an artist. His often bawdy tavern and household narratives were packed with hidden messages (red stockings for prostitution, oysters for sexual liaison, broken eggshells for mortality), creating allegories with a moral purpose.

6 Jacob van Ruisdael

Born in Haarlem, Jacob van Ruisdael (1629–1682), though not highly regarded in his own day, has come to be seen as one of the finest landscape and seascape painters of the Dutch school. His works are filled with restless skies and naturalistic details. Even calm scenes such as *The Windmill at Wijk* have a sense of dramatic grandeur.

For more on Dutch paintings See pp12–19

Pieter Claesz

7 As well as portraits, genre paintings and landscapes, still lives had an important place in Dutch 17th-century art. Peter Claesz (1597–1661) reached a peak of technical skill in his harmonious if academic compositions, which are replete with symbolic detail.

Vincent van Gogh

8 A troubled genius who left a vast body of work, despite his tragically short life *(see p19)*.

Piet Mondriaan

9 Although he lived in London, Paris and New York (and few of his works are on show in Amsterdam), Mondriaan was born and grew up in Holland (1872–1944). A leading member of the De Stijl movement, he created an abstract style using the simplest elements: straight lines and blocks of primary colour, arranged on the canvas to create harmony and balance.

Karel Appel

10 Karel Appel (1921–2006) was one of the founders of the CoBrA movement, started in 1948, which combined expressionist, abstract and surrealist influences *(see p128)*. His colourful works display a savage, forceful directness combined with an almost childlike optimism. "I paint like a barbarian in a barbarous age", he said.

Children with Dog by Karel Appel

Top 10 Dutch Literary Figures

1 Desiderius Erasmus
Scholar and humanist (1466–1536). Friend of Thomas More, no friend of Luther.

2 Hugo Grotius
Statesman and philosopher (1583–1645). Author of *De Jure Belli et Pacis*, the foundation stone of international law.

3 Gerbrant Bredero
Satirical poet and playwright (1585–1618), best known for *De Spaanse Brabander*.

4 Joost van den Vondel
Important playwright and poet (1586–1679) famed for his ornate style. Author of *Gijsbrecht van Amstel*.

5 Jan Six
Poet, playwright (1618–1700) and friend of Rembrandt, who painted his portrait.

6 Baruch Spinoza
Philosopher (1632–77) expelled by Amsterdam's Jewish community for his secular beliefs.

7 Multatuli
Pen name of Eduard Douwes Dekker (1820–87), whose work in colonial Java inspired his best-known novel *Max Havelaar*.

8 Anne Frank
Teenage victim (1929–44) of the Holocaust. Her eloquent diary has sold in its millions.

9 Gerard Reve
Novelist (1923–2006) influenced by his Catholicism and his homosexuality.

10 Cees Nooteboom
Prolific man of letters (b.1933) whose fiction is at best observant and poignant, at worst experimental and elusive.

Left **Joods Historisch Museum** Right **Jodenbuurt**

Jewish Sights

1 Anne Frank House
The plight of Jews like the Franks, forced into hiding by the Nazis, was brought to light by Anne's poignant diary; the house where they hid for 25 months is now a museum *(see pp32–3)*.

2 Joods Historisch Museum
This remarkable museum represents all aspects of Judaism and the history and culture of the Jews who settled in the Netherlands. On show are some marvellous paintings by Jewish artists, fascinating displays about the diamond industry, and exhibits that bring home the true horror of the Holocaust *(see p78)*.

3 Portugees-Israëlitische Synagoge
Inspired by the Temple of Solomon in Jerusalem, Elias Bouman's bulky red-brick synagogue is still the core of the small Sephardic community for whom it was built in 1675. The massive wooden barrel-vaulted ceiling is lit by more than 1,000 candles *(see p78)*.

4 Jodenbuurt
When the Jews arrived in Amsterdam in the late 16th century, they moved into a lacklustre area to the east of Oude Zijde, around present-day Waterlooplein. Although several synagogues, diamond factories and street markets have survived, the heart of the Jodenbuurt was decimated by post-war redevelopment and the building of the Metro. ◈ *Map Q5*

5 De Dokwerker
Mari Andriessen's evocative bronze statue (1952) is a memorial to the dockers' and transport workers' strike of February 1941 over the arrest of 450 Jews for the killing of a Nazi sympathizer. The event is commemorated every 25 February. ◈ *Jonas Daniel Meijerplein • Map Q5*

De Dokwerker

6 Hollandsche Schouwburg
Jewish families were rounded up at this operetta theatre before being transported to the death camps. A moving memorial and a small exhibition of memorabilia keep their memory alive *(see p125)*.

Hollandsche Schouwburg Monument

Interior of the Tuschinski Theater

Tuschinski Theater
This extraordinary 1921 theatre was the creation of its obsessive owner, Abraham Tuschinski, a Jewish emigré who died at Auschwitz. The sumptuous interior crosses Art Deco with the Orient *(see p108)*.

Ravensbrück Memorial
Dedicated to the women of Ravensbrück, one of the most disturbing of the city's Holocaust memorials (1975) incorporates a sinister soundtrack and flashing lights. ◎ *Museumplein • Map C6*

Verzetsmuseum Amsterdam
The Dutch Resistance Museum's brilliant displays give a vivid sense of life in an occupied country, as well as an insight into the ingenious activities of the Dutch Resistance. Exhibits include photographs, heart-rending letters thrown from deportation trains, film clips and room sets *(see p124)*.

Nooit Meer
In stark contrast to its peaceful surroundings, Jan Wolkers' Auschwitz memorial *Never More* features a slab of shattered glass. The fragments reflect a distorted view of the heavens, mirroring the damage done to humanity by the Holocaust. ◎ *Wertheimpark • Map R5*

Top 10 Jewish Historical Events

1 1592 onwards
Sephardic Jews from Portugal and Spain, fleeing the Inquisition, settle in Amsterdam, attracted by the city's religious tolerance.

2 1630s
Ashkenazi Jews start to arrive from eastern Europe (mainly Poland and Germany).

3 1796
Jews are given equal civil rights during Napoleon's Batavian Republic.

4 1860
Drawn to Amsterdam by its new industries and housing, Jews emigrate from Antwerp.

5 1932–7
These years see the rise of the Dutch Nazi Party under Anton Mussert; they also see waves of Jewish immigration from Hitler's Germany.

6 1941
In February, nine months into the German Occupation, the dockworkers strike in protest at the arrest and round-up of 450 Jews.

7 1942
The deportation of the Jews to Nazi death camps begins. Many Jews, including Anne Frank's family, go into hiding. Of the 80,000 living in pre-war Amsterdam, only 5,000 will survive the war.

8 1945
Amsterdam is liberated by Canadian troops on 5 May.

9 1947
Anne Frank's diary is published *(see pp32–3)*.

10 1975
Violent protests break out against the destruction of the Jodenbuurt – the old Jewish Quarter – in the Nieuwmarkt.

Left **Het Blauwe Theehuis** Right **De Taart van M'n Tante**

Cafés

De Jaren
Wood, air, glass and light seem the building elements of this spacious, multi-levelled grand café. Have a leisurely leaf through international newspapers at the reading table, pile up your plate at the salad bar, or sun yourself beside the canal on one of the best terraces in town (see p86).

Café de Jaren

Royal Café De Kroon
Elegance with an eclectic touch, the Royal Café De Kroon was named for the coronation of Queen Wilhelmina in 1898. The latest incarnation includes deep over-stuffed chairs and a large balcony. The restaurant serves some of the finest, affordable Dutch/International cuisine in town. Enjoy cocktails and salsa dancing on Wednesdays and Sundays.Thursday, Friday and Saturday nights are DJ nights.
⊗ Rembrandtplein 17 • Map N6
• 020 625 2011 • www.dekroon.nl

Greenwoods
Take a break from sight-seeing in this English-style tearoom with a charming atmosphere. Hearty all-day breakfasts, dainty high tea complete with cream cakes and a top notch selection of hot drinks make Greenwoods a popular hangout (see p86).

De Bakkerswinkel
Refined cream teas, delicate sandwiches, scrumptious cakes and mouthwatering quiches all baked on the premises. This huge, high-ceilinged lunchroom is suitable housed in an old tea warehouse. ⊗ Zeedijk 37
• Map Q2 • 020 489 8000 • Polonceau-kade 1 (Westerpark) • 020 688 0632
• www.debakkerswinkel.com

Het Blauwe Theehuis
"The Blue Teahouse" in the middle of the Vondelpark is a 1930s architectural treasure, a trendy night spot and a great terrace café all in one. Snack on well-filled sandwiches under the trees, dine in the upstairs restaurant or just stop by for a coffee on your walk through the park (see p119).

Walem
Sip a champagne cocktail on the canal-side terrace, or indoors with the fashionable crowd at one of Amsterdam's most popular cafés. Piles of magazines and intriguing artworks help while away the time (see p102).

 Recommend your favourite café on traveldk.com

De Taart van M'n Tante

My Aunt's Cake is the campest tearoom in town and is run by couture cake creators who supply Amsterdam's elite, including the mayor and the Dutch royal family. ✆ *Ferdinand Bolstraat 10 • Map D6 • 020 776 4600*

Pacific Parc

Inhabiting a vast industrial building on the grounds of a former gas works, this characterful café has Wi-Fi access, an open fire in winter and canalside terrace in summer. DJs feature Thu–Sun. ✆ *Polonceaukade 23 • Map C1 • 020 488 7778 • €€€*

1e Klas

A station café? If that gives you the horrors, think again. A minute or two in this stunningly decorated, classy 19th-century former first-class waiting room, and you're transported back in time. Station bustle becomes part of the atmosphere. ✆ *Platform 2b, Amsterdam Centraal Station, Stationsplein • Map P1 • 020 625 0131*

Tis Fris

A few steps from the Waterlooplein Flea Market *(see p63)*, this light and spacious split-level café serves healthy quiches, salads and soups as well as alcohol. A perfect mid-shop pitstop. ✆ *St Antoniesbreestraat 142 • Map Q4 • 020 622 0472 • €*

1e Klas, Centraal Station

Top 10 Types of Café

Bruin Café
Snug, smoky and old-fashioned, these brown cafés are the perfect places for beer and gossip.

Grand Café
Always grand in size, sometimes these cafés are grand in style too.

Eetcafé
Eetcafé means, unsurprisingly, Eat Café, and eat is exactly what you do in one. Good cooking at a little below restaurant prices.

Hip Hangouts
Some cafés flash their designer credentials – and attract a suitably hip and trendy crowd.

Music Cafés
Live music or top DJs make a good start to an evening of clubbing *(see pp54–5)*.

Games Cafés
Devotees of billiards, chess, darts or board games will find entire cafés given over to single pursuits.

Coffee & Cake
Sometimes there's no alcohol at all, just tea, coffee and more calories than you'd care to mention.

Nachtcafés
When all else is closed, these night cafés open their doors through the wee hours, though tread carefully – some may be a little seedy.

Gay Cafés
From the stylish to the sweaty, Amsterdam's famous gay cafés cater to all tastes.

"Coffeeshops"
Here, intoxicants take a different form, and smoking rather than drinking is the predominant activity.

For more cafés See pp80, 81, 86, 87, 94, 97, 105, 113, 118, 119

Left **Freddy's Bar** Right **Getto**

TOP 10 **Bars**

1 EVE
Step into the very upmarket, warm ambience of EVE. Modelled on the feel of a grand hotel lobby, with 1950s style leather banquettes, dark woods and a large, sleek, open fireplace, EVE offers a wide range of delicious and exotic finger food including lamb skewers and vegetarian tempura. Wednesday is "cocktail EVE", where you can sample a toffee martini. Live DJs Wed–Sun.
Ⓢ *Reguliersdwarsstraat 44 • Map M6 • 020 221 7070 • www.eve-amsterdam.com*

2 Brouwerij 't IJ
Adjacent to a landmark 1814 windmill and within a former bathhouse, this micro-brewery produces excellent local beer. There is a tour of the brewery every Friday, Saturday and Sunday. Regular and seasonal beers can be enjoyed at the tasting house and sunny terrace until 8pm. Ⓢ *Funenkade 7 • Map H4 • 020 622 8325 • 3–8pm daily*

3 The Minds
An old-school punk bar, with combat boots and battered skateboards hanging from the rafters, The Minds is different to the usual, trendy club scene. It has good beer, loud music and a pool table, if you're up to competing with the locals.
Ⓢ *Spuistraat 245 • Map M4 • 020 623 6784*

4 Barney's Uptown
Classy Barney's Uptown, part of the Barney's coffeeshop chain, boasts a good range of beers and spectacular cocktails and is smoker-friendly. It has half-price wine, and cocktails are available on Ladies' Night on Thursdays after 7pm. Ⓢ *Haarlemmerstraat 105 • Map D2 • 020 427 9469*

5 Prik
While the name of this extremely popular gay bar may sound rude, it's actually Dutch for "carbonation", with a nod to their signature drink – Prosecco on tap. "Spicy mango" is a favoured cocktail with tourists and locals alike (though Prik remains essentially Dutch). Monday brings cheap pints, and on Friday and Saturday DJs pump commercial house and pop music in the rainbow-neon interior.
Ⓢ *Spuistraat 109 • Map M2 • 020 320 0002 • www. prikamsterdam.nl*

XtraCold

For more bars **See pp80, 86, 87, 94, 97, 102, 110, 118**

Wijnand Fockink

Wijnand Fockink

6 *Proeflokalen*, the "tasting houses" of local distilleries, were once places to knock back a quick *jenever* (Dutch gin) before re-emerging into the winter's air. Crooked and cosy, with wooden barrels lining the walls, this one dates back nearly 400 years. Drop in for a quick one *(see p80)*.

XtraCold

7 For polar conditions beyond an Amsterdam winter, XtraCold offers a 4-D experience (3-D film with live effects, like the wind whipping through your hair) at −10 degrees Celsius. The bar requires pre-booking online, and around €20 buys you 45 minutes in the all-ice environment, with film, thermals, gloves and glasses, and one drink. Recover in the warm lounge bar with tapas and cocktails. ⚲ *Amstel 194–6 • Map P6 • 020 320 5700 • www.extracold.com*

Getto

8 Getto is a welcome relief to the screaming neon of the Red Light District. The owners claim it as an "attitude free zone", resulting in a very mixed clientele. Liberating and friendly, with a simple, home-style menu served in the evenings *(see p86)*. *Warmoesstraat 51 • Map P2 • 020 421 5151 • www.getto.nl*

Freddy's Bar

9 A favourite haunt of the late Alfred "Freddy" Heineken, Freddy's Bar attracts the A-list who flock to its leather banquettes to savour cocktails, gourmet nibbles and live music. ⚲ *De L'Europe, Nieuwe Doelenstraat 2–14 • Map N5 • 020 531 1707*

Café De Koe

10 Downstairs, people are tucking in to good, basic food; upstairs, they're shoulder to shoulder around the bar. Order a beer and you're instantly part of a no-nonsense neighbourhood bar atmosphere, with just a touch of merry mayhem, and everyone aiming headlong at a good night out. ⚲ *Marnixstraat 381 • Map K6 • 020 625 4482*

Left **Winston International** Right **Paradiso**

Clubs

Tonight (Arena Hotel)
The under-30s and super trendy flock to this hugely popular former orphanage, on the eastern side of the city, to dance to Amsterdam's top DJs. There are two floors, two separate dance areas, painted ceilings and marble arches. Regular nights include "Swingbeatz" (urban and R&B) every Friday and "Salsa Lounge"on the last Sunday of the month. ✪ *'s Gravesandestraat 51 • Map G5 • 020 850 2400 • www. hotelarena.nl*

Escape
One of Amsterdam's biggest and most exciting clubs, which can hold up to 1,300 people, has a huge dance floor, hi-tech lighting and as you would expect, a stunning sound system. At weekends it attracts a big out-of-town crowd. ✪ *Rembrandtplein 11–15 • Map N6 • 020 622 1111 • www.escape.nl*

Odeon

Odeon
A stunning combination of historic Amsterdam and sophisticated modern style, the Odeon is a venue for private parties, dinners and concerts throughout the week and a nightclub at weekends. The ultra-chic interior is within a building that dates back to 1662 by one of the city's loveliest canals. ✪ *Singel 460 • Map M5 • 020 521 8555 • www.odeontheater.nl*

Melkweg
This large, rambling multi-media centre housed in an old milk factory just off Leidseplein, is one of the country's top venues for live bands. Club nights, the hottest DJs, after parties, avant-garde theatre, art-house films, a gallery and eatery happily coexist under one roof. Admission varies *(see p57).*

Sugar Factory
Whether its avant-garde performances, sultry jazz or German electro nights, this club by the Leidseplein never fails to deliver an impressive programme. ✪ *Lijnbaansgracht 238 • Map K6 • 020 627 0008 • www.sugarfactory.nl*

Jimmy Woo
With its opulent interior, state-of-the-art sound system, superb lighting and celebrity clientele, Jimmy Woo is Amsterdam's most glamorous club. ✪ *Korte Leidsedwarsstraat 18 • Map K6 • 020 626 3150 • www.jimmywoo.com*

Paradiso

Formerly a church, now predominantly a live music venue, DJs spin here after the bands have been on – with an emphasis on Alternative music. The programming for parties can be erratic – anything from Moroccan dance nights to cinema-club evenings *(see p105)*.

Sugar Factory

Bar Bump

Gay/mixed, kitsch and fun. Thursday is "Popcorn" night, with drinks and fresh, free popcorn delivered on skates to the beat of pop music. DJs spin deep grooves, nu-disco and funky electro on Friday and Saturday. Happy hour from 6–8pm. Sunday is "Happy Landings" – liquid refreshments served via "trolly dollies". Free entry. 🅂 *Kerkstraat 23 • Map L6 • www.barbump.nl*

AIR

AIR maintains an intimate atmosphere thanks to its flexible layout. The club boasts state-of-the-art sound and visual systems, and offers a diverse programme for various tastes. 🅂 *Amstelstraat 16 • Map P6 • 020 820 0670 • www.air.nl*

Winston International

Eclectic and inspired programming give this small, rococo-style venue an edge on the city's other clubs. One of the best nights is "Cheeky Mondays", which is perfect for an indulgent start to the week. The club rocks to a drum 'n' bass beat until 4am, as well as live music (mostly rock 'n' roll) four nights a week. 🅂 *Warmoesstraat 131 • Map N3 • 020 623 1380 • www.winston.nl*

Left **Boom Chicago** Right **Tropentheater**

Performing Arts Venues

Muziekgebouw aan 't IJ
Amsterdam's spectacular concert hall for the 21st century opened in 2005. It occupies a unique position on a peninsula on the IJ, which gives it magnificent views. As well as a 735-seat main auditorium there is a smaller 125-seat hall, foyer decks overlooking the IJ and a café restaurant, the Zouthaven, with a waterfront terrace. The venue's impressive programme concentrates mainly on contemporary works. ◈ *Piet Heinkade 1 • Map G2 • 020 788 2000 • www.muziekgebouw.nl*

Boom Chicago
On a daily basis, this US comedy crew puts on satirical shows whose targets are anything from Dutch "quirks" to topical news issues. Big on laughs and big on beer. The latter, served in huge pitchers, is a welcome respite from the tiny frothy-headed *pilsjes*. Starwatchers note: Burt Reynolds once popped in. ◈ *Leidseplein Theater, Leidseplein 12 • Map K6 • 020 423 0101 • www.boomchicago.nl*

Het Bethaniën-klooster
The refectory of a former nunnery (dedicated to St Mary of Bethany) is now an intimate concert hall. The hall's size and acoustics are ideal for chamber music and jazz, and many leading international soloists and chamber groups perform here. ◈ *Barndesteeg 6B • Map P3 • 020 625 0078 • www.bethanienklooster.nl*

Carré
Originally built as a circus theatre in 1894, circus troupes still appear at this impressive landmark on the banks of the Amstel – along with anything from opera to ballet, magicians to music. Nothing beats sipping champagne on the balcony overlooking the river on a warm evening *(see p125)*.

Concertgebouw
The *crème de la crème* of international musicians and conductors appear at this palatial classical music venue – one of the world's most prestigious. Audrey Hepburn had a season ticket when she lived in Amsterdam, and it's not hard to understand why. Don't miss the free lunchtime concerts on Wednesdays *(see p115)*.

Concertgebouw

Stadsschouwburg

Het Muziektheater

The Dutch royals regularly pop in to catch shows at this comfortable – and once controversial – modern theatre, which is home to the Netherlands Opera and Ballet companies *(see p78)*. Tickets for shows – particularly opera – can sell out months in advance, so it's advisable to book before you travel. Inspired programming gives contemporary culture vultures an occasional look-in. ◉ *Waterlooplein 22 • Map Q5 • 020 625 5455 • www.het-muziektheater.nl*

Melkweg

This multimedia centre (the Milky Way) occupies a former dairy behind the Stadsschouwburg. Opened in 1970, the venue offers a wide range of entertainment including live music, film, theatre and dance. ◉ *Lijnbaansgracht 234A • Map K6 • 020 531 8181 • www.melkweg.nl*

Heineken Music Hall

Amsterdam's third-biggest live music venue (the ArenA next door, home to Ajax football team, is the biggest). Designed especially for amplified music, it has great acoustics and ambience during concerts. ◉ *Heineken Music Hall, ArenA Boulevard 590 • 0900 687 424 255 • www.heineken-music-hall.nl*

Stadsschouwburg

This Neo-Renaissance building – both of whose predecessors burned down – houses the city's municipal theatre. Local theatre groups, such as Toneelgroep Amsterdam, as well as visiting companies tread the boards here. The venue also hosts dance performances, most notably the annual Julidans (July Dance) Festival. ◉ *Leidseplein 26 • Map C5 • 020 624 2311 • www.ssba.nl, www.hollandfestival.nl*

Tropentheater

Eclectic world music/theatre performances are appropriately staged in the city's tropical museum *(see p127)*. You can also see some world cinema – but double-check the language the subtitles are in! ◉ *Mauritskade 63 / Linnaeusstraat 2 • Map G5 • 020 568 8500 • www.kit.nl*

Left **Patat** served with mayonnaise Right **Bitterballen**

Culinary Highlights

1 Maatjes Haring
Fresh raw herring, with chopped onion or gherkin, is sold as a snack from street stalls. Traditionally, you take your herring by the tail and toss it whole down your throat, with your head held back – but the faint-hearted may prefer them on a plate or in a roll. Best in May, when the *groene* (new season's) herrings appear.

2 Gerookte Paling
A delicious Dutch speciality, *paling* (smoked eel) comes from the IJsselmeer. Served with white toast and a squeeze of lemon, it makes a perfect starter.

3 Kaas
In the Netherlands, a staggering 14 kg (31 lb) of cheese per person is consumed each year. Gouda and Edam are the best known, but there are others, such as *Friese nagelkaas*, a clove cheese which became popular when spices were first imported in the 17th century.

4 Bitterballen
Served much like tapas to accompany drinks in a café or bar, these deep-fried meatballs have a crunchy exterior and a hot soft meat filling. They are served with mustard.

5 Hutspot
The Dutch love affair with potatoes manifests itself in a variety of hearty winter dishes. *Hutspot* (meaning hotchpotch) is a stew of braised beef and potatoes mashed with carrots, while *stamppot boerenkool* consists of mashed potato and cabbage flecked with chopped bacon and served with smoked sausage.

6 Erwtensoep
Like raw herring, this pea soup is another Dutch favourite that some foreigners find hard to love, with a consistency akin to wallpaper paste. Usually served with rye bread and smoked "raw" bacon. ✎ *Nieuwezijds Voorburgwal 5 • Map N1*

Erwtensoep

7 Rijsttafel
A delicious culinary after-echo of Holland's colonial past, Indonesian cuisine is usually eaten in the form of *rijsttafel* (rice table), a veritable feast consisting of as many as 25 little dishes of meat, fish, vegetables and sauces (some very hot), centred around a shared bowl of rice or noodles. Amsterdam has several good Indonesian restaurants, including Kantijl en de Tijger and Tujuh Maret *(see p61)*. ✎ *Kantijl en de Tijger: Spuistraat 291 • Map M4*

Appelgebak

Puddings are very popular, particularly the classic apple pie, accompanied by a large dollop of whipped cream *(slagroom)*. By common consent, the best *appelgebak* in Amsterdam is served at Winkel. ⊙ *Winkel: Noordermarkt 43 • Map D2*

Pannenkoeken

Pannenkoeken

Pancake houses offer an astonishing variety of fillings – try the Pancake Bakery *(see p97)* for an excellent selection. The traditional Dutch favourite is a large pancake topped with a thick syrup called *stroop*. If you have room for more, there are delicious, sugary *poffertjes*, the mini pancakes sold in summer from brightly painted stalls and from permanent stands at Dam Square and Leidseplein.

Patat

Served from street stalls in a handy paper cone, *patat* (chips) are ubiquitous, and very good indeed. They are generally made from whole (not pulped) Dutch potatoes, and fried in good, clean fat. Served with a large dollop of mayonnaise, they are definitely not for the diet-conscious. For the very best, go to Vleminckx. ⊙ *Vleminckx: Voetboogstraat 33 • Map M5*

Top 10 Drinks

1 Pils

The national drink of the Netherlands is beer. *Pils* – top brands Heineken and Grolsch – is the lager-like beer served (with froth) in bars. The Dutch generally drink it from small glasses, so it remains ice-cold to the last drop.

2 Witbier

Wheat-brewed white beer is pale and cloudy – often served with a slice of lemon.

3 Bokbier

A brown, sweet, winter beer served in round glasses.

4 Jonge Jenever

Dutch gin is flavoured with juniper and drunk neat – usually downed in a swift gulp from a small glass. *Jonge* (young) *jenever* is colourless and sharp.

5 Oude Jenever

Smoother, more complex, and slightly yellow in colour. Both types are referred to in bars as *borrel* (a tot).

6 Kopstoot

Aptly named, a *kopstoot* (head knock) is a *pils* swiftly followed by a *jenever* chaser.

7 Naveltje Bloot

Literally, Naked Tummy Button: a fruit liqueur traditionally taken when a mother-to-be shows off her bump to family and friends.

8 Oranje Bitter

An orange-flavoured liqueur knocked back on *Koninginnedag* (30 April).

9 Bakkie

A cup of strong black coffee, the way the Dutch prefer it.

10 Koffie Verkeerd

If you like your coffee milky, "wrong coffee" is what to ask for.

Left **Daalder Eten & Drinken** Right **Mamouche**

Restaurants

1 Supperclub
Dine while you relax on large white comfy beds, and enjoy a night's sensory experience to accompany your meal. Avant-garde performance, live DJs, art and entertainment are served up alongside five courses from a "World" kitchen not afraid to experiment. Supperclub Cruises on the canal combine lounge, dine and dance. ○ *Jonge Roelensteeg 21 • Map M3 • 020 344 6400 • www.supperclub.com • €€€€€*

2 Van Vlaanderen
The decor may be plain, but the dishes are rich and elaborate at this gourmands' paradise, for years known only to insiders until the restaurant acquired a number-one Zagat rating. Expect to feast on goose-liver, suckling pig, pigeon breasts, sweetbreads and other delightfully wicked fare. ○ *Weteringschans 175 • Map E5 • 020 622 8292 • €€€€*

3 Lof
Tantalizing aromas from the open-plan kitchen, clanging pans and cheery banter fill the air at this friendly, bistro-style local favourite. Amsterdammers in the know come for scrumptious, imaginative cooking, taking pot-luck from a set menu that changes daily. ○ *Haarlemmerstraat 62 • Map D2 • 020 620 2997 • Open Tue–Sat • €€€*

4 Daalder Eten & Drinken
A traditional Dutch-style Brown Café with a spacious terrace overlooking the Lindengracht. Daalder serves fresh, local food at reasonable prices. A favourite of locals and those looking to escape the more touristy commercialized city centre. ○ *Lindengracht 90 • Map D2 • 020 624 8864 • €€€*

5 Bridges
The sleek, modern look of the Grand Hotel's restaurant was inspired by Karl Appel's huge 1949 mural, *Seeking Children*, crowning the restaurant's entrance. Chef Aurélien Poirot, specializing in seafood accompanied by seasonal, locally sourced, organic vegetables, delivers nothing but the finest. ○ *Oudezijds Voorburgwal 197 • Map N4 • 020 555 3560 • www. bridgesrestaurant.nl • €€€€€*

Lof

For more restaurants See pp80, 81, 86, 94, 95, 102, 103, 110, 111, 113, 118

Bazar

6 Bazar

A lofty, former church provides a stunning home for this fantastic Eastern-influenced restaurant. Located along Albert Cuypmarkt *(see p109)* and decorated with colourful tables and lanterns, Bazar is a great place to dine after a day browsing the myriad market stalls. Expect delicious North African, Iranian and Middle Eastern delights *(see p111)*.

7 Tujuh Maret

Treating yourself to an Indonesian *rijsttafel* ("rice table") is an absolute must in Amsterdam – and this one is outstanding. Enjoy a feast of 18 deliciously spicy dishes, from mild to explosively chilli-filled, flavoured with coconut and ginger, peanuts and lemongrass, all served with mounds of rice. ⊗ *Utrechtsestraat 73 • Map E5 • 020 427 9865 • €€€*

8 Mamouche

Join a super-fashionable crowd in super-chic surroundings to experience the very best of Moroccan and French cuisine. Familiar dishes like lamb tagine and couscous share the menu alongside the chef's much more elaborate and exotic creations, such as the delicious stewed rabbit and sesame with baked apricots and cinnamon seeds. ⊗ *Quellijnstraat 104 • Map D6 • 020 670 0736 • €€€*

9 De Kas

You cannot get fresher or more locally sourced food than at the stunning greenhouse restaurant De Kas. Under its high glass ceiling, diners nestle among organic herbs and vegetables grown by Michelin-starred chef (and owner) Gert-Jan Hageman. The menu, prepared by head chef Ronald Kunis, is a three-course menu that changes with the seasons. Worth the trip. ⊗ *Kamerlingh Onneslaan 3 • 020 462 4562 • www.restaurantdekas.nl • €€€€€*

10 Hemelse Modder

Reservations are essential at this friendly, off-the-beaten track restaurant, renowned for its imaginative French- and Italian-influenced international cuisine and choice wine list. Besides attentive service, its best kept secret is its charming alleyway terrace. Fixed-price menus and vegetarian options available. ⊗ *Oude Waal 11 • Map Q3 • 020 624 3203 • €€€€*

Left **Bloemenmarkt** Right **Looier Kunst en Antiekcentrum**

Shops and Markets

1 Albert Cuypmarkt

Amsterdam's largest general market runs all the way down this long street in the Pijp area, touting everything from fresh fish to footwear. Come here for fabrics, but don't come here for clothes *(see p109)*.

Albert Cuypmarkt

2 Albert Heijn

Albert Heijn is a rather upmarket supermarket chain – there's at least one in each area of town. A little pricey, but the selection is wide, the aisles are wide, and they're wide awake: unusually, several centrally located branches stay open until 10pm. ✆ *Various branches*

3 De Bijenkorf

Named "The Beehive" (which just about sums it up if you're here at the weekend), Amsterdam's prestigious department store caters for everyone from children to clubbers. Often described as the Dutch Harrods, prices ensure

that it's only the well-monied who tend to part with their cash here. ✆ *Dam 1 • Map N3*

4 Bloemenmarkt

Amsterdam's famous floating flower market – the stalls still float, but now they are permanent *(see p108)*.

5 HEMA

This ubiquitous, cheap and cheerful department store chain started life in 1926 and has become something of a Dutch institution. The store offers affordable designer products, practical clothing, stationery, kitchen equipment and food products. It also stocks its own brand of items. ✆ *Various branches*

6 Boerenmarkt

Amsterdam's organic Saturday "farmer's market" is a treat rather than a routine shopping trip. Cruise the stalls to the accompaniment of some fine busking and sample free goats' cheese and other goodies – plus freshly-baked bread, flowers and a fabulous fungi selection. ✆ *Noordermarkt • Map D2*

7 Looier Kunst en Antiekcentrum

Burrow for bargains in this highly browsable and perpetually intriguing indoor warren of antiques and collectibles. When you come up for air, there's also a café where you can put your weary feet up *(see p100)*.

Magna Plaza

Built between 1895 and 1899, this magnificent building – once derisively dubbed "post-office Gothic" by its critics – was designed by Cornelis Hendrik Peters (1874–1932) to house Amsterdam's head post office. Now a shopping mall, around 40 diverse stores are located over its four floors. There are two cafés. ◈ *Nieuwezijds Voorburgwal 182 • Map M3*

Noordermarkt

There has been a market on this site since 1627 – a fact you can contemplate as you fight over the bargains with the die-hard clubbers who arrive here after a night out, or with the locals who come for a more civilized Monday-morning rummage. Unbeatable for second-hand clothes and accessories *(see p92)*.

Waterlooplein

Whether your taste is exotic crafts and jewellery or vintage clothes, you can find them from Monday to Saturday at the city's best flea market – although it's a jumble at the best of times. When you can take no more, escape to the adjacent indoor markets. ◈ *Map Q5*

Magna Plaza

Top 10 Souvenirs

1 Beer
There's more to Dutch beer than Heineken. The Dutch make a fabulous variety of beers, and you will find many of them at De Bierkoning *(see p87)*.

2 Bulbs
Check your country's import regulations before packing this fabulous floral souvenir into your luggage.

3 Cannabis
Don't even think about it.

4 Cheese
If you don't have time to make it to an out-of-town cheese market, visit De Kaaskamer *(see p104)* for a mouth-watering selection that's guaranteed to impress more than Edam or Gouda.

5 Clogs
The quintessential Dutch footwear; be in fashion, and be heard.

6 Condoms
Novelty condoms galore, and in a variety of flavours; the city's infamous Condomerie will oblige *(see p81)*.

7 Delftware
If you don't manage to snag one of the dishy Dutch, at least you can take home a Dutch dish.

8 Diamonds
Definitely a girl's best friend, but possibly the worst nightmare of the poor guy who has to fork out for them.

9 Jenever
"The father of gin" – the real thing, in a variety of flavours and bottle types.

10 T-shirts/Postcards
No shortage of T-shirts and postcards portraying anything from the utterly sublime to the absolutely ridiculous.

For more shops **See pp81, 87, 104, 105, 112, 113, 119**

Left **The Jordaan from the tower of the Westerkerk** Right **Leidseplein by night**

Walks and Cycle Rides

Jordaan
Start at Westerkerk (see p91), perhaps climbing its tower for a bird's-eye view of the area. Work your way north to picturesque Brouwersgracht (see p92).

Shopping Walk
Beginning at Noordermarkt (see pp63, 92), take Prinsengracht to the Negen Straatjes (see p100) with its quirky shops. Have a look at De Looier antiques market in Elandsgracht (see p62) before heading down Lijnbaansgracht to Leidseplein. Turn up Leidsestraat and make for Metz & Co, with its top-floor café (see p99) – then on to Bloemenmarkt (see pp63, 108), ending at De Bijenkorf on Damrak (see p62).

Nightlife Walk
Start at the entertainment hub, Leidseplein (see p101), before moving to the bright lights around Rembrandtplein (see p107). Wind down at the junction of Reguliersgracht with

The Oudeschans

Herengracht, where you can see no less than 15 romantically lit bridges. Continue to Amstelkerk, finishing in Utrechtsestraat, with its many appealing cafés and restaurants (see p61, 110, 111).

Around Oudeschans
From Centraal Station, discover a quiet part of the old city by taking Binnenkant, lined with fine houses, and then, passing Montelbaanstoren, walking along Oudeschans to reach the Rembrandthuis (see p77). Pause at De Sluyswacht, the crooked café on the bridge (see p80), before exploring the old Jewish quarter, Jodenbuurt (see p48), or continuing to Nieuwmarkt (see p77).

Herengracht
Shortest and most fascinating of the Grachtengordel (see pp8–11), the Herengracht is lined with beautiful buildings, such as Bartolotti House (Nos 170–172), the Bijbels Museum (see p99) and the mansions of the Golden Bend (see p8).

To Ouderkerk aan de Amstel
For a tranquil cycle ride, follow the Amstel from the city centre (start near Blauwbrug) to Ouderkerk aan de Amstel (see p128). The route passes Amstelpark and the De Rieker windmill (see p127) before entering attractive countryside. About 20 km (12 miles) round trip.

7 Plantage

With its distinguished villas, tree-lined streets, parks and gardens, Plantage *(see pp122–5)* is a calm district to explore by bike (with the exception of busy Plantage Middenlaan).

8 Prinsengracht

At 3 km (2 miles), the outermost canal of the Grachtengordel *(see p8)* is quite tiring on foot, but makes a very pleasant, fairly carfree cycle ride, with plenty of cafés at which to rest along the way.

9 Western Islands

Perhaps the most peaceful part of Amsterdam in which to walk or cycle lies to the north-west of Centraal Station. The islands of Prinseneiland, Bickerseiland and Realeneiland, together known as the Western Islands, have a remote, bracing quality, with well-worn boatyards and white drawbridges, as well as modern housing *(see p93)*.

10 Amsterdamse Bos

This attractive wooded park south of the city is ideal for cyclists, thanks to 48 km (30 miles) of cycle path; those on foot have no less than 160 km (100 miles) of footpath to stroll along. Perfect for a family picnic outing *(see p128)*.

Prinsengracht

Top 10 Tips for Cycling in Amsterdam

1 Stick to the Rules
Don't copy the locals, who frequently jump red lights and ride on sidewalks.

2 Stay in the Cycle Lanes
Amsterdam has an excellent integrated network of *fietspaden* (cycle lanes), with white lines, cycle signs and dedicated traffic lights.

3 Cross Tramlines with Care
If you have to, cross tramlines at an angle, to avoid your front wheel getting stuck.

4 Avoid Trams
They are bigger than you, and can't be steered; listen for their rattle and stay clear.

5 Watch for Pedestrians
It's usually tourists who mistakenly walk in cycle lanes; keep an eye out for parked cars, too.

6 Give Priority
Motorists and cyclists have priority when entering your road from the right.

7 Dismount at Busy Junctions
Unless you are really confident, it's better to negotiate these on foot.

8 Don't Cycle Two-Abreast
It's only allowed if you are not obstructing the traffic; otherwise, stay in single file.

9 Use Lights
By law, you must turn your lights on after dusk – you must also have reflector bands on both wheels.

10 Lock Your Bike
Bicycle theft is rife. Make sure that you always lock both front wheel and frame to an immovable object.

Amsterdam's Top 10

 For information on bicycle hire **See p135**

Left **De Star Hofje** Right **Egelantiersgracht**

Places for Peace and Quiet

1 De Star and Zon's Hofjes
These two charming court-yards, just a few paces from each other, offer the weary visitor a retreat from the crowds. ✆ *Prinsengracht 89–133 & 159–71 • Map D2*

2 Museum Van Loon
Behind Adriaan Dortsman's grand façade, the Van Loon family residence has a calm, welcoming feel. Lose yourself in the intimate, elegantly furnished rooms, or in the charming rose garden with its 18th-century coach house disguised as a Classical temple *(see pp30–31)*.

18th-century sledge, Museum Van Loon

3 Zandhoek
Only a few minutes away from the bustle of central Amsterdam, Zandhoek (on Realeneiland in the Western Islands) feels remote and slow-paced. Cobbles, white draw-bridges, 17th-century buildings and splendid old barges moored along the harbour front make a picturesque sight *(see p93)*.

4 Binnenkant
Bordering Waalseilands-gracht, an attractive side-canal dotted with houseboats, Binnenkant is lined with fine old merchants' houses. A couple of well-placed benches at the junction with Kalkmarkt allow you to sit and contemplate a charming stretch of the Oudeschans, site of the city's first shipyards, and the fortified Montelbaanstoren towering above it *(see p79)*. ✆ *Map Q3*

5 Café de Sluyswacht
A few steps down from busy Jodenbreestraat brings you to the crooked Café de Sluyswacht *(see p80)* with its spacious terrace, where tables and chairs are set out at the merest hint of fine weather. A surprisingly tranquil spot, from here you enjoy a different perspective of the Oudeschans.

6 Grimburgwal
This peaceful corner of the Oude Zijde at the convergence of three canals was a popular spot for medieval convents: appropriately, one of the side streets is called Gebed Zonder End (Prayer Without End). If you need to rest, there are benches on Oudezijds Voorburgwal, just beyond the Huis op de Drie Grachten. ✆ *Map N5*

Hortus Botanicus
A wild and verdant place dotted with tropical palmhouses and welcome benches, the small botanical garden on the east side of the city dates back to 1682, when an apothecary's herb garden was established here *(see p124)*.

Bijbels Museum Garden
Behind the Bible Museum is a tranquil formal garden that is full of plants mentioned in the Bible. The garden is a lovely spot to rest after visiting the museum; there is a café on site serving tea, coffee and other refreshments *(see p99)*.

Egelantiersgracht
The Westerkerk carillon might be the only sound to break the silence as you stroll along this pretty side-canal in the Jordaan bordered by artisans' dwellings. At Nos 105–141, St Andrieshofje, built in 1616, is one of the city's oldest and best preserved almshouses. A charming blue-and-white tiled passage leads from the street into the courtyard *(see p92)*. Ⓝ *Map J2*

Overloopplantsoen
This sleepy little park nestles at the junction of two canals, Nieuwe Keizersgracht and Plantage Muidergracht. Ⓝ *Map R6*

Hortus Botanicus

Top 10 Vantage Points

1 Westerkerk Tower
Climb Amsterdam's tallest tower to see the attractive jumble of the Jordaan below *(see p91)*.

2 Zuiderkerk Tower
The top of the tower gives a vista of the former Jewish quarter *(see pp42 & 81)*.

3 Oude Kerk Tower
See the medieval city and the red-light district from this tower *(see p29)*.

4 Metz & Co
The city's most impressive canal views are from the sixth-floor café and the cupola perched on top *(see p99)*.

5 Madame Tussauds Amsterdam
The round window on the top floor offers a terrific view of Dam Square *(see p35)*.

6 Amstelveld
From this peaceful square at the junction of Reguliersgracht and Prinsengracht, there are pretty stretches of the canal in both directions.

7 Magere Brug
Stand on this bridge at night for splendid views of the Amstel *(see p11)*.

8 Reguliersgracht and Herengracht
Put Thorbeckeplein behind you and count 10 bridges from this junction – a spectacular sight after dark.

9 OBA
The seventh-floor terrace of the Amsterdam Public Library on Oosterdokseiland offers superb city views *(see p134)*.

10 NEMO
Climb the broad outside stairs to the roof for a striking view across the Oosterdok to the city *(see p68)*.

Amsterdam's Top 10

Sign up for DK's email newsletter on traveldk.com

Left **Artis Zoo** Right **NEMO**

🔟 Children's Attractions

1 East Indiaman Amsterdam
A splendid replica of a Dutch East India Company ship that sank on its maiden voyage in 1749. Watch the sailors hoisting cargo and swabbing decks. The ship is moored outside Het Scheepvaartmuseum *(see p123)*, where it has been since it was built in 1991.

East Indiaman Amsterdam

2 The Little Orphanage
Visitors to The Little Orphanage children's exhibition at the Amsterdam Museum, can experience what life was like in a 17th-century orphanage. Children are sent on engaging quests to find hidden animals in the house, or discover more about an orphan boy, Jurriaan *(see pp24–7)*.

3 Tram Rides
Go to Haarlemmermeer railway station and then take a 20-minute ride in an old-fashioned tram with wooden seats, clanging bell and friendly conductor to Amsterdamse Bos, where you will find pancakes, peacocks, and plenty of leg-stretching space. ◎ *Electrische Museumtramlijn: Haarlemmermeer-station, Amstelveenseweg 264 • 020 673 7538 • www.museumtramlijn.org • Trams depart Apr–Oct: 11am–5:30pm Sun • Admission charge*

4 Westerpark
With entertainment for kids and parents alike, this cultural park has an arts complex, Sunday markets, outdoor wading pool, playgrounds, children's farm, Het Woeste Westen natural adventure park, and plenty of cafés to boot. ◎ *Children's farm: 023 682 2193 Open 9am–5pm Tue–Sun • Woeste Westen: Open 11am–6pm Wed, Sat & Sun; 1–6pm Mon, Tue, Thu & Fri • www.woestewesten.nl*

5 NEMO
It's worth going to the science and technology centre for the building alone – dubbed "Titanic" – and for the superb views you can get from the top deck. Inside, enquiring minds will be kept alert with experiments and demonstrations *(see p129)*.

6 Artis Royal Zoo
Children love this action-packed zoo, where they can pat the animals in the children's farm, brave the steamy reptile house, see stars in the planetarium, and marvel at the fish in the aquarium *(see p123)*.

7 Vondelpark

Together with the Westerpark, this is the perfect place to go with kids on a summer's day. It has a paddling pool, playgrounds, Kinderkookkafé (Kids Café) and a children's atelier on Wednesday afternoons (at the Groot Melkhuis), *(see p115).*

8 TunFun

This vast indoor adventure playground occupies a disused underpass. Parents can sit back and relax as pre-teens run wild in the warren of tunnels, slides and trampolines, while toddlers romp in their own special area. ⊗ *Mr Visserplein 7 • Map Q5 • 020 689 4300 • Open 10am–6pm daily • Closed 1 Jan, 30 Apr • Admission charge*

9 Tropenmuseum

Learn about the cultural diversity of Africa, or pour over Dutch colonial history in this museum dedicated to ethnography and contemporary art. Tropenmuseum Junior, the "hands on" museum for children (ages 6 to 13), is open by appointment, with tours in Dutch, or English by special request *(see p123).*

10 Madame Tussauds Amsterdam

Surprizing, educational and, at times, emotional encounters with superheroes and film stars are to be had here. There's a great view of Dam Square from the round window, too *(see p35).*

Tropenmuseum Junior

Top 10 Sights and Sounds for Free

1 Civic Guards Gallery

Huge portraits of the Civic Guard at the Amsterdams Historisch Museum *(see p26).*

2 Begijnhof

A haven of peace and tranquillity right in the centre of the city *(see p22–3).* For more delightful *hofjes* in the Jordaan, *see p92.*

3 De Hollandsche Manege

Stylish 19th-century royal riding school *(see p117).*

4 Rijksmuseum Garden

Architectural curiosities in a formal garden *(see p14).*

5 Lunchtime Concerts

At the Concertgebouw every Wednesday at 12:30pm, September to June *(see p119)* and at the Boekmanzaal in the Stadhuis *(see p78)* on Tuesdays at 12:30pm, October to June.

6 Ferry across the IJ

Join the locals on the 5-minute ferry ride from Centraal Station *(see p84)* to North Amsterdam or to the NDSM wharf (15 minutes).

7 Bloemenmarkt

Locals and tourists alike love the Singel's colourful floating market *(see p108).*

8 Seven European Houses

See Europe in a minute at Roemer Visscherstraat 20–30a – a row of houses in the style of seven countries *(see p148).*

9 Barrel Organs

A joyful feature of Amsterdam's streets – there are eight of them in all.

10 Church Bells

The carillons of the Westertoren, Zuidertoren and Munttoren unleash their glorious peals, from noon–1pm Tue, Thu & Fri respectively.

Left **Koninginnedag** bric-a-brac sale Right **Koninginnedag** revellers

Festivals and Events

1 Nationaal Museumweekend
Most of Amsterdam's state-run museums participate in this scheme, run by SMK (Stichting Museumkaart), to offer free or reduced-price entry for one weekend. Details are published through the Tourist Board in mid-March. ● *mid-Apr*

2 Koninginnedag
On Queen's Day – the late Queen Juliana's birthday – the whole city becomes a gigantic street party. The locals sell bric-a-brac on the streets, public stages are set up all around the city, and people dressed in orange throng the streets. Music blares all day, and the party goes on till dawn. ● *30 April*

3 Bevrijdingsdag
The day after *Herden-kingsdag* (Remembrance Day), Liberation Day celebrates the end of the Nazi occupation with speeches, concerts and open-air markets in the Vondel-park, Leidseplein, Museumplein and Rokin. ● *5 May*

4 Holland Festival
An exciting programme of theatre, music, opera, musical theatre and art at various venues in the city, the Holland Festival has earned itself a prestigious reputation, attracting top-flight performers from the Netherlands and abroad. ● *020 788 2100 • www.hollandfestival.nl • Jun*

5 Open Monumentendagen
An exciting opportunity to see what lies behind the gabled façades and medieval doorways of some of the city's most historic buildings, which are open to the public for free over this weekend. ● *020 422 2118 • www.openmonument endag.nl • Second weekend in Sep*

6 Open Tuinendagen
During Open Garden Days some 30 canal house gardens are open to the public. Visit the green spaces of several museums, like Van Loon *(see pp30–31)*, and take the rare opportunity to see many private gardens. A day ticket includes transport by canal boat to all houses. ● *Third weekend in Jun • www.opentuinendagen.nl*

7 Grachtenfestival
National and international stars perform classical music concerts at several locations around Grachtengordel during this 10-day festival *(see p11)* .

Traditional dancers at the Jordaan Festival

Prinsengrachtconcert, Grachtenfestival

The highlight is a free piano recital given on a barge on Prinsengracht opposite the Pulitzer Hotel. Concerts are also held at Muziekgebouw aan't IJ *(see p56).* ✆ *020 421 4542* • *www.grachtenfestival.nl* • *Aug*

Jordaan Festival
This picturesque district *(see p92)* makes an ideal setting for a low-key early-autumn festival. The local talent comes out of the woodwork for contests on Westermarkt, with concerts, street parties and fairs – like the one devoted to food in Noordermarkt *(see pp92 & 97).* ✆ *Sep*

Sinterklaas' Parade
The Christmas festivities start here. St Nicholas, the Dutch Santa Claus, arrives near St Nicholaas Kerk by steamboat with his mischievous servants, *Zwarte Pieten* (Black Peters). Together, they distribute sweets and gifts to the children of Amsterdam. ✆ *Second or third Sat in Nov*

Vondelpark Openluchttheater
Each summer, Vondelpark's open air theatre, located in the heart of the park, plays host to a series of free concerts and performances, including dance, music, children's theatre and comedy *(see p119).* ✆ *www. openluchttheater.nl* • *Jun–Aug*

Top 10 Spectator Sports

1 Football
See Ajax at their remarkable 50,000-seater stadium. ✆ *Amsterdam ArenA, Bijlmer* • *Aug–Dec, Feb–May*

2 Cycling
The RAI Derny Race is Amsterdam's only criterium (road circuit). ✆ *Amsterdam RAI, Europaplein* • *mid-May*

3 Rugby
AAC Rugby Club caters for all ages ✆ *Bok de Korverweg 6* • *Apr–Jun*

4 Korfbal
A cross between netball and basketball. Blauw Wit is the club to watch. ✆ *Sportpark Joos Banckersweg* • *Sep–Jun*

5 Hockey
Amsterdamsche Hockey & Bandy Club are the ones to watch. ✆ *Nieuwe Kalfjeslaan 19, Amstelveen* • *Sep–May*

6 Ice Hockey
The city supports the popular Amstel Tigers. ✆ *Sporthal Jaap Edenhal, Radioweg 64* • *Oct–late Mar*

7 American Football
If you can't get tickets to watch Ajax, the Amsterdam Admirals also play at the ArenA *(see above).* ✆ *Mar–Jun*

8 Running
Popular runs are the Dam tot Damloop and Amsterdam Marathon. ✆ *Olympisch Stadion Stadionplein* • *Sep–Oct*

9 Rowing
Popular among the numerous competitions is the Head of the Amstel River race. ✆ *Last week Mar*

10 Show-jumping
Jumping Amsterdam is a series of international indoor competitions. ✆ *Amsterdam RAI, Europaplein* • *Jan–Feb*

Left **Haarlem** Right **Hortus Botanicus, Leiden**

🔟 Excursions

1 Aalsmeer Bloemenveilingen

Witnessed from an elevated viewing gallery, the world's largest flower auction is an astonishing sight. With flowers, speed is of the essence, and the atmosphere is frenetic. Bidding is highly automated, using the "backwards" Dutch clock system: the clock counts down (and prices lower) until a buyer stops the clock and wins the auction.
🕸 www.floraholland.com

2 Delft

Sleepy Delft was shaken by a gunpowder explosion in 1654, after which the town was rebuilt – as recorded in *A View of Delft* by Vermeer around 1660. Since then, little has changed. There are Delft tiles in the Museum Lambert van Meerten and the shops. In Het Prinsenhof are the bullet holes left by the murder of William of Orange; his mausoleum is in the Nieuwe Kerk. 🕸 www.delft.nl

3 The Hague

Political capital of the Netherlands, Den Haag (The Hague) is a stately city, with many public buildings and lovely parks. Centred round the Gothic Ridderzaal, places of interest include the parliament buildings, the International Court of Justice and the Mauritshuis, elegant home of the superlative Royal Picture Gallery. The seaside resort of Scheveningen is not far away. 🕸 www.denhaag.nl

4 Enkhuizen

The fortunes of this attractive former fishing port declined dramatically after the construction of the huge Afsluitdijk in 1932 created the freshwater IJsselmeer and cut it off from the North Sea. Today it is home to the wonderful Zuiderzeemuseum, which includes a reconstruction of a typical fishing village with costumed "inhabitants" and craftsmen at work.

5 Haarlem

Centred around the Grote Markt, with its buzzing pavement cafés and lovely buildings, the historic centre of this lively, well-heeled city is a delight. Highlights include the Frans Hals Museum, the Grote Kerk with its magnificent decorated Müller organ, and the Art Deco train station. The Teylers Museum has an excellent collection of science, technology and art exhibits. 🕸 www.visithaarlem.org

Lime kilns, Zuiderzeemuseum, Enkhuizen

*Visit the Aalsmeer flower auction website at www.floraholland.com
Visit the Zuiderzeemuseum website at www.zuiderzeemuseum.nl*

Keukenhof
Throughout spring, but climaxing in mid-April when the tulips flower, a drab coastal strip between Leiden and Haarlem bursts into colour. Among these commercial bulbfields is the wooded Keukenhof park, a dazzling and unforgettable sight between late March and late May.
❧ www.keukenhof.nl

Leiden
An easy-going university town, full of cycling students, Leiden offers plenty of canals, cafés and museums, as well as the lovely Hortus Botanicus.
❧ www.portal.leiden.nl

Marken
Just 16 km (10 miles) from Amsterdam, this former island fishing community, now reached by a narrow causeway, makes a refreshing day trip. Its distinctive wooden houses are charming.

Paleis Het Loo
Built in 1686 by Stadholder William III as a hunting lodge, Het Loo was a royal summer residence until the 1960s. A sober façade belies a sumptuous

Wooden house, Marken

interior, with rooms decorated to reflect different eras, from the 1680s to the 1930s. There are also superb formal gardens to enjoy.
❧ www.paleishetloo.nl

Utrecht
Like Leiden, Utrecht is a university city with much to offer – notwithstanding the vast, unappealing Hoog Catherijne shopping complex. A major medieval religious centre, it still has many traces of its past, and a lovely historic town centre.
❧ www.utrechtyourway.nl

Visit the Frans Hals Museum website at www.franshalsmuseum.nl
Visit the Paleis Het Loo website at www.paleishetloo.nl

AROUND TOWN

AMSTERDAM'S TOP 10

Left **Stopera** Right **Museum Het Rembrandthuis**

Oude Zijde

THE STREETS OF THE OUDE ZIJDE (OLD SIDE) *are packed with historic and beautiful buildings, though many are buried in the seediest parts. As the name suggests, this is where Amsterdam has its roots; the city grew from a ribbon of land on the eastern bank of the Amstel between Damrak and Oudezijds Voorburgwal (which means "before the city wall"). Today, the Oude Zijde incorporates the medieval city, built around the Oude Kerk, and the area to the east, where development started in the 15th century and continued over the following two centuries to accommodate Jewish émigrés. An area of richness and contrasts, within its boundaries lie the Nieuwmarkt* (dominated by the Waag, a 15th-century city gate turned weigh-house), the university quarter, Chinatown, the Red Light district, and what remains of the old Jodenbuurt (see p48), where four former synagogues have been combined to form the superb Joods Historisch Museum.

Oude Kerk

Sights

1 Oude Kerk
2 Nieuwmarkt
3 Museum Het Rembrandthuis
4 Zeedijk
5 Red Light District
6 Stopera
7 Joods Historisch Museum
8 Portugees-Israëlitische Synagoge
9 Hash Marihuana & Hemp Museum
10 Montelbaanstoren

Previous pages **Neck-gable buildings overlook houseboats moored against the side of a canal in the Grachtengordel**

The Waag, Nieuwmarkt

Oude Kerk
The oldest church in Amsterdam has been altered and extended over the years, producing a heavenly jumble of architectural styles from medieval to Renaissance *(see pp28–9)*.

Nieuwmarkt
This vast open square has been a marketplace since the 15th century, and is still the scene of a weekly organic market each Saturday. Alone in the middle stands the bulky Waag (1488), bristling with turrets. The eastern gate in the city's defences, it was originally called St Antoniespoort. In the 17th century it became a weigh house and home to numerous guilds, including the surgeons'. It was here that Rembrandt painted his famous *Anatomy Lesson of Dr Tulp*. There were few problems acquiring bodies for dissection, since public executions took place in the Nieuwmarkt. ⊕ *Map P3*

Museum Het Rembrandthuis
Using the detailed inventory drawn up at Rembrandt's bankruptcy in 1658, the museum has been reconstructed to look just as it did in the artist's time. Of special interest are pictures by his master, Pieter Lastman. One room contains exotic collectibles

of the day – spears, shells, Roman busts – as well as Rembrandt's precious art books and record of his effects *(see p15)*. Etching and paint-making demonstrations enhance the experience. ⊕ *Jodenbreestraat 4 • Map Q5 • 020 520 0400 • www.rembrandthuis.nl • Open 10am–5pm daily • Closed 1 Jan, 30 Apr, 25 Dec • Admission charge*

Zeedijk
Built in the early 1300s, the Zeedijk (sea dyke) was part of Amsterdam's original fortifications. As the city grew the canals were filled in and the dykes became obsolete. At No. 1 is one of the city's two remaining wooden-fronted houses, dating from the 16th century. Opposite is St Olofskapel, built in 1445 and named for the first Christian king of Norway and Denmark. ⊕ *Map Q2*

Red Light District
The world's oldest profession occupies Amsterdam's oldest quarter, De Wallen, bordered by Zeedijk, Kloveniersburgwal, Damstraat and Warmoesstraat. Today, it is one of the city's greatest tourist attractions and a campaign to make the area more attractive was launched in 2007. The council has confined window-prostitutes to two main areas, and encouraged small creative businesses to open up shop in their place. ⊕ *Map P2, P3*

Red Light District

Stopera

6 With the Dutch penchant for clever wordplay, the Stadhuis-Muziektheater is better known as "Stopera" because it combines the *stadhuis* (town hall) with the headquarters of the city opera and ballet companies. This red brick, marble and glass building was built in 1987 amid intense controversy, since scores of medieval houses, among Jodenbuurt's few remnants, had to be destroyed in the process. In the passage between Stopera's two buildings, a bronze button indicates the exact NAP (*Normaal Amsterdams Peil*) water level. 🌑 *Waterlooplein 22 • Map Q5 • Stadhuis: 14 020 • Open 8:30am–noon Mon–Fri (Arcade open 8am–midnight daily) • Muziektheater: 020 625 5455*

Joods Historisch Museum

7 Abel Cahen's prize-winning design for the Jewish Historical Museum (1987) is a perfect marriage of old and new: the four synagogues that house it, built by Ashkenazi Jews during the 17th and 18th centuries, are linked by glass-covered internal walkways. Located in the heart of the old Jewish quarter, this multimedia museum explains the history and culture of the Jewish community

Joods Historisch Museum

in the Netherlands. Younger visitors will enjoy the Children's Museum *(see pp48–9)*. 🌑 *Nieuwe Amsterdam 1 • Map Q5 • 020 531 0310 • www.jhm.nl • Open 11am–5pm daily • Closed Yom Kippur, Rosh Hashanah • Admission charge*

Portugees-Israëlitische Synagoge

8 The Sephardic Jews, who settled in Amsterdam from the late 16th century, celebrated their new lives in a tolerant society a century later by commissioning Elias Bouman to build this imposing synagogue. It follows a traditional design with the Hechal (Holy Ark), facing Jerusalem, opposite the tebah, from where the cantor leads the service *(see p48)*. 🌑 *Mr Visserplein 3 • Map R5 • 020 624 5351 • www.portugese synagoge.nl • Open Apr–Oct: 10am–4pm Sun–Fri; Nov–Mar: 10am–4pm Sun–Thu, 10am–2pm Fri • Closed Sat & Jewish hols • Admission charge*

Hash Marihuana & Hemp Museum

9 Exhibits in this fascinating museum chart the history of hemp (marijuana) from its earliest use some 8,000 years ago to the 20th-century drug wars. As *hennep*, it was used in the Netherlands for making lace, linens, fishing nets and fabric for sails, and processed by special wind-

Modern-day Tolerance

In line with Amsterdam's long tradition of tolerance, the authorities generally overlook the personal possession and consumption of small quantities of cannabis or marijuana, although they are illegal. Their sale and use at regulated coffeeshops *(see p51)* is officially accepted, but hard drugs and advertising are not. In 1990, brothels and the display of girls in their windows were legalized, although street prostitution remains illegal.

mills called *hennepkloppers*. There are displays about smuggling, an array of hookahs and reefers, and a "grow room" where plants are cultivated.
⊗ *Oudezijds Achterburgwal 148 • Map P3 • 020 624 8926 • www.hashmuseum. com • Open 10am–11pm daily • Admission charge*

10 **Montelbaanstoren**
A fortified tower, the Montelbaanstoren was built in 1512 on the eastern edge of Amsterdam, just outside the city wall. Its original purpose was to defend the Dutch fleet; now, more prosaically, it houses the Amsterdam water authority. The open-work steeple was added by the ubiquitous Hendrick de Keyser in 1606, when the city fathers felt that they could at last afford the icing on the proverbial cake. It overlooks the lovely Oudeschans (see p64), a canal that also dates from the early 16th century, dug to improve access for ships.
⊗ *Oudeschans 2 • Map R3*

Montelbaanstoren

A Day in the Oude Zijde

Morning

As the Oude Kerk does not open until 11am, start your day with a tour of the **Museum Ons' Lieve Heer op Solder** (see pp20–1). Although in the Nieuwe Zijde, it is only a few steps from the **Oude Kerk** (see pp28–9), which you can visit afterwards. Then walk to **Nieuwmarkt** (see p77) for a break at In de Waag (Nieuwmarkt 4), where you can sit, overlooking the square, in summer. Afterwards, make your way to Oudezijds Achterburgwal for the **Hash Marihuana & Hemp Museum** (see p78). Then follow the main drag of the **Red Light district** (see p77), Oudezijds Voorburgwal, as far as Bridges Restaurant (see p60) for lunch.

Afternoon

Walk down to peaceful Grimburgwal and the House on the Three Canals. Agnietenkapel (now closed) is a few doors away. From here, head east to Oudezijds Achterburgwal and cut through Oudemanhuispoort (stone spectacles mark the entrance), browsing through the second-hand bookstalls as you go. Continue to Jodenbreestraat and the **Museum Het Rembrandthuis** (see p77). After your tour – if it is a Monday, Wednesday, Friday or Saturday – pop into Pintohuis (see p44) for a glimpse of the painted ceiling. Revive yourself in Café de Sluyswacht (see p80). From here there is a lovely canalside walk, past the **Montelbaanstoren**. Turn left and stroll along Binnenkant before heading back to your hotel.

Left **Wijnand Fockinck** Right **In 't Aepjen**

Restaurants, Cafés and Bars

Bird
Those in the know flock here for the tastiest Thai in town. Eat in their restaurant or duck out to their snackbar opposite for an utterly authentic experience. ✎ *Zeedijk 72 • Map P2 • 020 620 1442 • €€*

Café Cuba
An intriguing ode to the communist country, this long and narrow, darkly-lit bar serves fantastic cocktails and pitchers of sangria. There is a pool table at the back. ✎ *Nieuwmarkt 3 • Map P3 • 020 627 4919*

In 't Aepjen
This unusual bar is located in one of the oldest wooden houses in the city (1551). Sailors would pay for their stay in monkeys – hence the primate theme. ✎ *Zeedijk 1 • Map P2*

De Bekeerde Suster
In 1544, the nuns at this cloister started making beer, a tradition revitalized a few years ago – and there's a fine restaurant. ✎ *Kloveniersburgwal 6-8 • Map P4 • 020 423 0112*

Café de Sluyswacht
Rembrandt sketched this leaning ex-lock-keeper's house. It has a lovely canalside terrace at the back. ✎ *Jodenbreestraat 1 • Map Q4 • 020 625 7611*

De Engelbewaarder
Frequented by hi-brow locals, this convivial bar serves cheap and cheerful food and specialist beers on a peaceful canalside terrace. Live jazz on Sundays. ✎ *Kloveniersburgwal 59 • Map P4 • 020 625 3772*

VOC Café
Housed in the city's oldest defence tower, the Schreierstoren (*see p10*), this traditional-style bar has a "reading room" and two terraces overlooking the water. ✎ *Prins Hendrikkade 94 • Map Q1 • 020 428 8291*

Wijnand Fockink
Barely looking a day older than its 1679 origins, this is the best *proeflokaal* (tasting house) in town. The hidden garden out back is only for use by guests of the Krasnapolski Hotel. ✎ *Pijlsteeg 31 • Map N3 • 020 639 2695*

Lime
One of the hippest and friendliest bars in the area. ✎ *Zeedijk 104 • Map P3 • 020 639 3020*

Blauw aan de Wal
An absolute treasure in the heart of the Red Light District, this European restaurant should be savoured. ✎ *Oudezijds Achterburgwal 99 • Map P4 • 020 330 2257 • €€€€*

Recommend your favourite restaurant on traveldk.com

Price Categories

For a three-course
meal for one with half
a bottle of wine (or
equivalent meal), taxes
and extra charges.

€	under €20
€€	€20–€30
€€€	€30–€45
€€€€	€45–€60
€€€€€	over €60

Latei

☜10 Best of the Rest

1 Condomerie
A huge, hilarious range of (mostly) novelty condoms guaranteed to spice up the most jaded of love lives. ☜ Warmoesstraat 141 • Map N3

2 Fo Guang Shan Temple
This nun-run Chinese Buddhist temple takes pride of place on Zeedijk. Take a respectful peek one afternoon (you can keep your shoes on), or join a tour, held Saturday afternoon. ☜ Zeedijk 106-118 • Map P3 • 020 420 2357 • €

3 W139
Founded in 1979, W139 has evolved from its artist-run squat, anti-establishment roots to become a professional platform for contemporary art. ☜ Warmoesstraat 139 • Map N3 • 020 622 9434 • www. w139.nl • Open noon–6pm Mon–Sun

4 Jacob Hooy & Co
Established in 1743, this is the best place in town to pick up herbs, homeopathic remedies, teas and essential oils. ☜ Kloveniersburgwal 10–12 • Map P3

5 Joe's Vliegerwinkel
Colourful kites, quirky knick-knacks and kitsch bits for that perfect present to suit all ages. ☜ Nieuwe Hoogstraat 19 • Map P4

6 Latei
A delightful café cum bric-a-brac store. Ideal for a sandwich, fresh juice and decent-sized coffees. ☜ Zeedijk 143 • Map P3

7 Beestenwinkel
Toys, gadgets and games with an animal theme. From squirting fish to cuddly bears and rubber ducks that glow in the bath. ☜ Staalstraat 26 • Map P5 • www.beestenwinkel.nl

8 Droog Design
A group of young Dutch designers have joined forces to form Droog Design. Check it out for witty home accessories and furniture. ☜ Staalstraat 7A/B • Map P5 • www.droog.com

9 Tibet
Quite a find in the seedy surrounds of the Red Light District, this restaurant serves food until midnight. ☜ Lange Niezel 24 • Map P2 • 020 624 1137 • €

10 De Zuiderkerk
Built 1603–11 by Hendrick de Keyser, painted by Monet in 1874. Climb to the top for great views. ☜ Zuiderkerkhof 72 • Map P4 • 020 552 7987 • Church open 9am–5pm Mon–Fri, noon–4pm Sat. Free • Closed public hols • Tower open 1–5pm Mon–Sat, Apr–Sep • Admission charge

Left **Koninklijk Paleis** Right **View across Dam Square to the Nieuwe Kerk**

Nieuwe Zijde

DESPITE ITS NAME, THE NIEUWE ZIJDE (NEW SIDE), *together with the Oude Zijde, was at the centre of Amsterdam's early maritime settlement. From the boundary between the two districts, the Nieuwe Zijde extends west to the Singel. Its canal pattern once mirrored that of its neighbour, but over time it developed an entirely different character. The medieval city, with its wooden housing, was highly susceptible to fire, and much of the area was burnt down in 1452, necessitating extensive reconstruction. During the 19th century, most of its canals were filled in; the resulting thoroughfares, Damrak, Rokin and Nieuwendijk, are lively shopping streets, as is Kalverstraat, scene of a medieval market. Despite the changes, pockets of history survive – in the network of narrow 14th-century streets off Kalverstraat, the Begijnhof, the 17th-century orphanage that houses the Amsterdam Museum, and, at the heart of the district, Dam Square.*

Monstrance (c.1700), Museum
Ons' Lieve Heer op Solder

🔟 Sights

1. Dam Square
2. Koninklijk Paleis
3. Nieuwe Kerk
4. Amsterdam Museum
5. Begijnhof
6. Museum Ons' Lieve Heer op Solder
7. Centraal Station
8. Beurs van Berlage
9. Allard Pierson Museum
10. Spui

Gilded cherub, Nieuwe Kerk

Dam Square
Amsterdam's main square is named after the dam on the River Amstel, around which the city grew. By the 17th century, it had become the focus of the Dutch trading empire (see pp34–5).

Koninklijk Paleis
Supported by a staggering 13,659 wooden piles, Jacob van Campen's Classical building occupies one side of Dam Square. Designed as the Stadhuis (town hall), it was transformed into a Royal Palace in 1808 by King Louis Bonaparte. Although it is still used for official functions, such as the wedding reception of Crown Prince Willem-Alexander in February 2002 (see p39), the present royal family live elsewhere. It is now open to the public (see p34).

Nieuwe Kerk
Wealthy merchant banker Willem Eggert donated his orchard as a site for this Gothic church, as well as a large sum of money for its construction. It was consecrated to Our Lady and St Catherine, but has only ever been called the Nieuwe Kerk – to distinguish it from the Oude Kerk. When the town hall became the royal palace in the early 19th century (see above), it was given the new, elevated title of national church of the Netherlands, and has been the setting for the coronation of every Dutch monarch since then (see p34).

Amsterdam Museum
An excellent place to start a visit to Amsterdam, this museum chronicles how a tiny fishing village on the Amstel river grew into one of the wealthiest and most beautiful cities in the world (see pp24–7).

Begijnhof
A charming and secluded courtyard of houses surrounding a tranquil garden in the centre of the city, the Begijnhof was established in the 14th century as a sanctuary for a lay Catholic sisterhood (see pp22–3).

Museum Ons' Lieve Heer op Solder
This canal house turned museum, with its sober decoration and delightful secret Catholic church (schuilkerk) hidden within, plunges the visitor back into the Golden Age (see pp20–1).

Amsterdam Museum collection

Centraal Station

Centraal Station

For many visitors, their experience of Amsterdam begins at Centraal Station, the transport hub of the city, where some 1,400 trains arrive and leave every day. It was built in the 1880s in Neo-Renaissance style by P J H Cuypers, who was also responsible for the Rijksmuseum *(see pp12–15)*, and A L van Gendt, designer of the Concertgebouw *(see p115)*. Before work on the building could start, three artificial islands had to be constructed and 8,600 wooden piles sunk to support them. The fact that the building blocked Amsterdammers' view of the sea caused much controversy at the time. The ornate red-brick façade depicts themes of travel, trade and city history, picked out in gold and other colours. If you have time, visit the station restaurant, 1e Klas *(see p51)*, to see its fine Art

Amsterdam's Colonial Past

Acknowledged during the 17th century as the most powerful city in the Netherlands, Amsterdam turned its sights overseas. Expeditions established a spice trade out of Indonesia, and in 1602 the Dutch East India Company (VOC) was founded, followed in 1621 by the Dutch West India Company. Dutch colonies in Brazil and on Manhattan Island eventually succumbed, respectively, to Portuguese and English sea-power.

Nouveau setting. Major renovation works mean that parts of the building are closed until 2015.
🜨 *Stationsplein • Map P1 • 0900 9292*

Beurs van Berlage

The innovative Stock Exchange building was derided when it was unveiled in 1903, but is now considered a key work of the period and almost universally admired. Designed by the pioneer of Dutch modern architecture, H P Berlage, its functional lines are softened by ornamental ironwork and tiled mosaics. The Stock Exchange has now moved next door, and Beurs van Berlage is the head office of the Nederlands Philharmonic Orchestra. It is used for exhibitions and contains a permanent display on the history of the Stock Exchange. Try to get a look at the amazingly light and spacious interior. 🜨 *Damrak 277*
• Map N2 • 020 530 4141 (exhibitions), 020 521 7500 • www.beursvanberlage.nl
• Open only during exhibitions
• Admission charge

Allard Pierson Museum

Located in a stately Neo-Classical house built in the 1860s as a bank, this delightful small museum was named after the University of Amsterdam's first Professor of Classical Archaeology, and contains its archaeological collection. Fascinating exhibits conjure up vivid pictures of life in ancient civilizations; they include Egyptian mummies and sarcophagi, Coptic clothes, Cypriot jewellery, Greek geometric and red-figured pottery, Etruscan metalwork and Roman glassware and statuary. A special exhibition space holds temporary exhibitions each year on different archaeological related subjects.

🖳 *Oude Turfmarkt 127 • Map N5 • 020 525 2556 • www.allardpiersonmuseum.nl • Open 10am–5pm Mon–Fri, 1–5pm Sat, Sun & public hols • Closed 1 Jan, Easter Sun, Whitsunday, 30 Apr, 25 Dec • Admission charge*

🔟 Spui

One of the most genial places in the city, this small square lined with cafés, bars and bookshops is generally quiet during the winter, but in summer, it bursts into life at lunchtime and again in the evening, when people spill out onto the pavement from bars. Cheek by jowl with university buildings, Spui has traditionally been a place where intellectuals gather to drink and debate. There is also a Friday book market. During the Provo riots of the 1960s *(see p39)*, the square was the scene of political protests and demonstrations, during which Carol Kneulman's twee statue of an urchin, *Het Lieverdje* (Little Darling) was frequently daubed with slogans. At No. 18, Café Hoppe *(see p86)* is a landmark brown café that has been in business since 1670.
🖳 *Map M5*

Het Lieverdje, Spui

A Day in the Nieuwe Zijde

Morning

🕙 Spend the morning in the **Amsterdams Museum** *(see pp24–7)*, although a morning is scarcely enough. When you feel like a break, leave the main building and head for the Kalverstraat entrance, where the café-restaurant David and Goliath is on your left. Make sure that you keep your ticket so that you can re-enter the museum without having to pay again. The end of the tour brings you to the excellent museum shop.

Rather than leaving by one of the exits, cut through the Civic Guards' Gallery to the **Begijnhof** *(see pp22–3)*, and while away some time in this secluded place. Come out of the Gedempte Begijnensloot entrance and turn the corner into **Spui**, where you might lunch at Café Hoppe *(see p86)* or Café Luxembourg (Spui 24).

Afternoon

After lunch, walk down Kalverstraat, the district's main shopping street, to Dam Square, where you could visit the **Koninklijk Paleis** as well as the **Nieuwe Kerk** *(see pp34–5)*. Then take a break among the tiny shops built into the buttresses of the church in Gravenstraat; at No.18, De Drie Fleschjes is one of the oldest *proeflokalen* (tasting houses), dating from 1650.

When you are revived, walk down Damrak past the **Beurs van Berlage** *(see p84)* to finish your day at the **Centraal Station**, where you can hop on a tram back to your hotel.

Left **De Jaren** Right **Supperclub**

Restaurants, Cafés and Bars

1 Café Restaurant Amsterdam

Housed in a 19th-century pump house, this industrial chic at its best, offering Dutch classics and fusion, accompanied by fine wines and free Wi-Fi. ⊘ *Watertorenplein 6 • Map B1 • 020 682 2666*

2 Keuken van 1870

A local favourite, this former soup kitchen dishes up homely meat and vegetarian dinners at bargain prices. ⊘ *Spuistraat 4 • Map N1 • 020 620 4018 • €*

3 Café Hoppe

Open since 1670, this historic brown café, with its lefty past and church pews, was a regular haunt of radical writers and intellectuals in the Provo-fuelled 1960s. ⊘ *Spui 18 • Map M5 • 020 420 4420*

4 De Jaren

Formerly a bank, this modern grand-café, with huge windows, serves sandwiches, soups and delicious meals. In summer, the waterside terrace is the place to be. ⊘ *Nieuwe Doelenstraat 20 • Map N5 • 020 625 5771*

5 Het Schuim

Art meets alcohol at this large, rustic-style bar, a popular hangout for creative types. Food served till 9:30pm. ⊘ *Spuistraat 189 • Map M3 • 020 638 9357*

6 Getto

This gay/straight/mixed bar *(see p53)* also has a restaurant open in the evenings serving home-style filling meals. Burgers are a speciality. ⊘ *Warmoesstraat 51 • Map P2 • 020 421 5151 • www.getto.nl • €€*

7 Greenwoods

Australian-run, English tearoom-style café that serves great breakfasts and high teas. Service can be slow, but worth the wait *(see p50)*. ⊘ *Singel 103 • Map M1 • 020 623 7071*

8 Supperclub

There's a decadent lounge bar in the basement of this hip restaurant. Dress to impress if you want to get in. ⊘ *Jonge Roelensteeg 21 • Map M3 • 020 344 6400*

9 Brasserie Harkema

A stylish establishment boasting a spacious dining room. Choose from the classic Parisian brasserie menu or come for late-night nibbles. Caters for groups. ⊘ *Nes 67 • Map N4 • 020 428 2222 • €€€*

10 Kapitein Zeppos

Tucked away in a tiny alleyway, this charming restaurant serves French cuisine with Mediterranean influences. ⊘ *Gebed Zonder End 5 • Map N4 • 020 624 2057 • €€€*

Recommend your favourite café on traveldk.com

De Bierkoning

Price Categories

For a three-course
meal for one with half
a bottle of wine (or
equivalent meal), taxes
and extra charges.

€ under €20
€€ €20–€30
€€€ €30–€45
€€€€ €45–€60
€€€€€ over €60

TOP 10 Best of the Rest

1 Café Gollem
This beer café serves a wide selection of pilsners, ales and stouts. Chalkboards crammed with tasty dishes and a comfortable wooden interior, make this a beer lover's paradise.
Raamsteeg 4 • Map M4

2 Het Japanse Winkeltje
Japanese crafts centre selling beautiful lacquered and china bowls, sake decanters and kimonos. *Nieuwezijds Voorburgwal 177 • Map M3*

3 The American Book Center
Three floors of books, magazines, newspapers and games. There are also art exhibitions, lectures and writers' workshops at the Treehouse annexe, a short walk away.
Spui 12 • Map M5

4 De Bierkoning
"The Beer King" in the shadow of the Dam's Royal Palace has a fantastic range of beers – almost 1,000 of them – from all over the world. *Paleisstraat 125 • Map M3*

5 DOM-CK
Hypertrendy fashion and interior shop from Germany, selling anything from moose scarves to retro bead curtains.
Spuistraat 281a–c • Map M4

6 P G C Hajenius
Dutchman Hajenius fulfilled his 1826 pipe dream, and his store is now one of Europe's most famous cigar houses. A must for all cigar connoisseurs, but worth a peek just for the Art Deco interior. *Rokin 92–6 • Map N3*

7 Profiles Hair & Body Spa
For an afternoon of pampering, head to this spa where therapists work to Ayurvedic principles. Offers haircare, manicures and pedicures. *Spuistraat 330 • Map M5 • 020 627 6337*

8 Puccini Bomboni
A chocoholic's paradise! Mouthwatering chocolates often with surprizing fillings, such as nutmeg, lemongrass or pepper. Real junkies can also feast on big chunks of chocolate bars. *Singel 184 • Map M2*

9 Gastronomie Nostalgie
This charming shop sells elegant tableware for special occasions. Stock includes silverware, porcelain and crystal. *Nieuwezijds Voorburgwal 304 • Map M4*

10 Bitterzoet
This modern club has music nights to suit everybody, from live bands to DJ sets. *Spuistraat 2 • Map N1 • 020 421 2318*

Following pages **View over the Prinsengracht**

Left **Eerste Klas Café, Centraal Station** Right **Prinsengracht**

Left **Café de Jaren** Right **Montelbaanstoren, Oudeschans**

 Following pages **façade of Zuiderkerk**

Left **Houseboat on Brouwersgracht** Right **Amsterdam Tulip Museum**

Western Canal Ring

FOR MANY, THE WESTERN CANAL RING *is the area of Amsterdam that perfectly encapsulates the city's relaxed yet stylish air. Construction of the Grachtengordel, Amsterdam's 17th-century ring of three fashionable canals (see p11), began here, with the marshy area just beyond reserved by city planner Hendrick Staets for workers and their unpalatable industries; Huguenot refugees who settled here – like others fleeing religious persecution – were said to have named it* jardin *(garden), later corrupted to Jordaan, and today it is one of Amsterdam's most fascinating – and bohemian – districts. Its narrow streets and oblique canals might seem random, but they followed the course of old paths and drainage ditches. North of the charming Brouwersgracht lies the revitalized district of Haarlemmerbuurt, and, further afield, the Western Islands, Bickerseiland, Prinseneiland and Realeneiland, created in the mid-17th century to provide much-needed warehousing.*

Huis met de Hoofden

🔟 Sights

1. Anne Frank House
2. Westerkerk
3. Homomonument
4. Huis met de Hoofden
5. Jordaan
6. Amsterdam Tulip Museum
7. Noordermarkt
8. Brouwersgracht
9. Haarlemmerbuurt
10. Western Islands

Anne Frank House

This thought-provoking museum encompasses the *achterhuis* – the secret hideout of Anne Frank and her family – as well as background information on the plight of Amsterdam's Jews and racial oppression *(see pp32–3)*.

Westerkerk

An exacting climb to the top of the soaring tower of Wester-kerk, a landmark close to the heart of every Amsterdammer, rewards you with a thrilling view *(see p67)*. Designed by Hendrick de Keyser and completed in 1631, its austere interior is un-adorned, except for the ornate organ and its lively painted shut-ters. A memorial to Rembrandt reminds us that he was buried here, although the precise burial site is unknown. Outside the church, notice the poignant, diminutive statue of Anne Frank and Homomonument, the pink granite triangle which commemorates persecuted homo-sexuals. ⊗ *Prinsengracht 281. Map L2. 020 624 7766. www.westerkerk.nl • Church: open Apr–Oct: 11am–3pm Mon–Fri (Jul–Aug also Sat). Free • Tower: open Apr–Oct: guided tours every 30 mins from 10am–6pm Mon–Sat (for further information call 020 689 2565) Admission charge*

Homomonument

This first memorial in the world to gay men and women who lost their lives during World War II, also pays tribute to homosexuals who are still being oppressed today. The memorial was designed by Dutch artist Karin Daan and was erected in 1987. It consists of three

Homomonument

equilateral triangles made of pink granite, one level with the street, one protruding into the Keizersgracht and one slightly raised – symbolising the past, present and future. The pink triangle, originally a badge gay men were forced to wear in the World War II concentration camps, became a symbol of gay pride in the 1970s and 80s.
⊗ *Westermarkt (between Westerkerk and Keizersgracht)*
• *Map L2 • Tram 13, 14, 17*
• *www.homomonument.nl*

Huis met de Hoofden

An eye-catching extravaganza, the House with the Heads is named for the six heads on its elaborate step-gabled façade representing Classical gods – Apollo, Ceres, Mars, Minerva, Diana and Bacchus. Built in 1622 for a successful merchant, its Dutch Renaissance design is attributed to Hendrick de Keyser. The ground floor has scarcely changed. ⊗ *Keizersgracht 123 • Map L2 • Closed to the public except on Monumentendagen (see p70)*

Westerkerk

Hazenstraat, Jordaan

Jordaan

Quirky and characterful, with an intimate, easy-going atmosphere all of its own, the Jordaan is a dense patch of small-scale streets and canals peppered with interesting shops and galleries, charming *hofjes* and inviting brown cafés. Bounded by Prinsengracht and Lijnbaansgracht to east and west, and Brouwersgracht and Looiersgracht to north and south, it was built for workers at the same time as the Grachtengordel (see p11). • *Map K3*

The Amsterdam Tulip Museum

Tulips were first introduced to the Netherlands in the late 16th century, starting a love affair that is still going strong today. The Amsterdam Tulip Museum is dedicated to telling the story of the "world's most dangerous flower", through exhibits documenting tulip cultivation and interactive displays that trace the history of the modern flower from its wild beginnings. Visitors can buy tulip memorabilia and have bulbs shipped to the US or EU countries. • *Prinsengracht 112* • *Map L2* • *www.amsterdamtulip museum.nl* • *Open 10am–6pm daily*

Noordermarkt

By the entrance to the Noorderkerk (see p42), a still-flourishing Protestant church, a sculpture commemorates the *Jordaanoproer* (Jordaan riot) of 1934, in which seven people died during demonstrations against cuts in unemployment benefits. Today the tranquil surrounding square, a market site since 1627, comes to life during the Monday flea market and the Saturday *boerenmarkt*, selling organic produce. • *Map D2* • *Noordermarkt flea market: 9am–1pm Mon* • *Boerenmarkt: 9am–4pm Sat*

Brouwersgracht

If you stand at the breezy junction of Brouwersgracht and Prinsengracht you will get terrific views in all directions. Today, Brouwersgracht, with its pretty bridges and picturesque houseboats, is a romantic's (and photographer's) delight, but if a 17th-century brewery (*brouwer*) worker could see it now, he would be astonished to find that the spout-gabled warehouses of this once reeking industrial canal had been converted into the smartest of private housing – particularly fine examples of which you can see at Nos 188–194. • *Map D1*

Zon's and De Star Hofjes

Secretive and intimate, Amsterdam's *hofjes* – almshouses for the needy built by wealthy merchants in the 17th and 18th centuries – are part of the city's charm. Unobtrusive street entrances lead to pretty houses, some of which are still used for their original purpose. Two of the most delightful *hofjes* are Zon's and De Star on the Prinsengracht (see p66). Both *hofjes* can be visited from Monday to Friday.

Haarlemmerbuurt

The bustling streets of this stalwart residential neighbourhood have seen the arrival of all manner of shops, mixing bric-a-brac with *haute couture*, New Age with funky furniture and specialist food with local groceries. On Haarlemmerstraat is Westindisch Huis, once the headquarters of the Dutch West India Company *(see p45)*. To the west is Haarlemmerpoort, a gateway – now converted into flats – built in 1840 for the entry of William II. Beyond it lies peaceful Westerpark *(see p68)* and Westergasfabriek, the former gasworks turned arts centre. ◉ *Map D1*

Western Islands

Despite being very much part of the city, the man-made Western Islands have a remote, bracing quality. Comprising Bickerseiland, Prinseneiland and Realeneiland, they were created in the early 17th century to accommodate shipyards and warehouses. Large-scale development has since taken place, and modern housing now co-exists in harmony with white wooden drawbridges. The area's many artists work from studios housed in warehouses, and open their doors to the public in May for the annual Open Ateliers Westelijke Eilanden. ◉ *Map D1*
• www.oawe.nl

Boatyard, Prinseneiland

Exploring the Western Canal Ring

Morning

🕐 Beat the queues and be first to arrive at the **Anne Frank House** *(see pp32–3)*, which opens at 9am. Afterwards, you could take a contemplative walk along Prinsengracht to the Western Islands, perhaps first climbing the tower of **Westerkerk** *(see p91)*. On the way, drop in on two peaceful *hofjes*, **Zon's** and **De Star** *(see facing page)*. For refreshment, visit ☕ Papeneiland, a tiny brown café founded in 1642, at the junction of Prinsengracht and Brouwersgracht.

On the **Western Islands**, stroll round Prinseneiland and along Zandhoek on Realeneiland, where you could lunch very well at De Gouden Reael (Zandhoek 14). If you are 🍴 with children, visit Dierencapel, the children's farm on Bickerseiland.

Afternoon

En route to the Jordaan, hardened shoppers will first want to stop in 🕐 **Haarlemmerbuurt**, with its mix of shops, both smart and tatty. Don't miss a peak at over-the-top Café Dulac (Haarlemmerstraat 118), and the world's narrowest restaurant, De Groene Lanteerne (Haarlemmerstraat 43).

Spend a couple of hours exploring the endlessly picturesque **Jordaan**, then join today's breed of young Jordaanese in one of the trendy cafés around Noordermarkt – Finch or ☕ Proust, or the wildly kitsch Café Nol in Westerstraat. If it's dinner time, head for 🍴 Manzano *(see p95)*, for good tapas and sangria.

Left **'t Smalle** Right **Café Finch**

Bars and Cafés

1 't Arendsnest
The place to discover Dutch beer, with over 350 varieties from 50 breweries and micro-breweries. Group tastings can be arranged via the website. ⊙ *Herengracht 90 • Map M1 • 020 421 2057 • www.arendsnest.nl*

2 Duende
Release the inner gypsy in this busy tapas bar in the Jordaan. Authentic atmosphere, value for money, and live Flamenco music. Olé! ⊙ *Lindengracht 62 • Map C2 • 020 420 6692 • €€*

3 Café Finch
This small watering-hole on the edge of a scenic square can get decidedly crowded. In summer, the hip local clientele spills out onto the square. ⊙ *Noordermarkt 5 • Map D2 • 020 626 2461*

4 Café P96
This peaceful bar opens around 8pm in the evenings and stays open later than most. The premises extend in the summer to an outdoors terrace on a fairy-lit barge. ⊙ *Prinsengracht 96 • Map L1 • 020 622 1864*

5 Harlem
This rustic café serves wholesome "soul food" plus hearty sandwiches and fruit shakes. ⊙ *Haarlemmerstraat 77 • Map D2 • 020 330 1498*

6 Stout!
Minimalist café drawing a hip crowd who come for the latest trends in international cuisine and the fine wines. ⊙ *Haarlemmerstraat 77 • Map D2 • 020 616 3664 • €€€*

7 't Smalle
Originally a liquor distillery, this brown bar is now a discerning wine-café. A must-see. ⊙ *Egelantiersgracht 12 • Map L1 • 020 623 9617*

8 Café Sound Garden
Don't let the tattoos, piercings and grunge factor put you off. This bar has a great atmosphere, a large waterside terrace and some unusual beers on tap, too. ⊙ *Marnixstraat 164–166 • Map J3 • 020 620 2853*

9 Tabac
Tabac used to be a brown café but has succumbed to the lounge trend. ⊙ *Brouwersgracht 101 • Map D2 • 020 622 4413*

10 Café de Twee Zwaantjes
Open from mid-afternoon until the early hours, The Two Swans is an authentic Jordaan bar. Enjoy a drink while you listen to accordion music, unique to this once working-class district. ⊙ *Prinsengracht 114 • Map L2 • 020 625 2729*

Price Categories

For a three-course meal for one with half a bottle of wine (or equivalent meal), taxes and extra charges.	€	under €20
	€€	€20–€30
	€€€	€30–€45
	€€€€	€45–€60
	€€€€€	over €60

Spanjer & Van Twist

🔟 Restaurants

1 Balraj
The sister of Beatrix, Queen of the Netherlands, is a regular diner at this well-priced restaurant offering some of the best Indian food in town. ◈ *Haarlemmerdijk 28 • Map D1 • 020 625 1428 • €€*

2 Lieve Belgian Restaurant
Satisfying, affordable Belgium cuisine, served up with fat, chunky Belgian chips. ◈ *Herengracht 88 • Map M1 • 020 624 9635 • www.restaurantlieve.nl • €€€*

3 De Bolhoed
Undoubtedly one of the most charming restaurants in the area. Delicious, well-priced vegetarian (and vegan) food with a wicked dessert selection. ◈ *Prinsengracht 60 • Map L1 • 020 626 1803 • €€*

4 Restaurant Christophe
Classically trained chef Jean-Joel Bonsens adds his own infusions to French classics such as caviar and blinis, or roasted leg of venison with salsify and juniper. ◈ *Leliegracht 46 • Map L2 • 020 625 0807 • €€€€€*

5 Foodism
Mediterranean cuisine for a decent price. The calamari and grilled marinated lamb are highly recommended. Friendly service. ◈ *Nassaukade 122 • Map B3 • 020 486 8137 • www.foodism.nl • €€*

6 Werck
A few doors down from the Anne Frank House (*see pp32–3*), this lounge-style establishment serves creative international dishes. ◈ *Prinsengracht 277 • Map K2 • 020 627 4079 • €€€*

7 Manzano
Reached through a court-yard, this authentic Spanish tapas restaurant offers a good, inexpensive menu and copious sangria. ◈ *Rozengracht 106 • Map K3 • 020 624 5752 • €€*

8 Spanjer & Van Twist
The perfect place to rest those weary feet. Hole yourself up for the afternoon in the second-floor window seat. ◈ *Leliegracht 60 • Map L2 • 020 639 0109 • €€*

9 Toscanini
Despite its quiet location and deceptive size (it's huge inside), this superb Italian restaurant gets quickly booked up. The cooks create delicious dishes from an open kitchen. ◈ *Lindengracht 75 • Map C2 • 020 623 2813 • €€€*

🔟 De Vliegende Schotel
Offering delicious vegetarian and vegan dishes, with a wide selection of organic wines and beers. ◈ *Nieuwe Leliestraat 162–8 • Map K2 • 020 625 2041 • €€*

→ Recommend your favourite restaurant on traveldk.com

Left **G.D.E. Jongejans** Right **Mechanisch Speelgoed**

TOP 10 Shopping

1 Back Beat
Jools Holland and even Mick Jagger have popped into this new and second-hand record/CD shop specializing in jazz, soul, funk and R&B. Rare collector's items to be had. ◎ *Egelantiersstraat 19 • Map L1*

2 Quinta
This quirky little wine store is the city's only one selling authentic Absinthe. Alternatively, try the traditional Dutch Jenever as well as wines on tap. Bring your own bottle or buy a cheap one at the store. ◎ *Niewe Leliestraat 4 • Map K2*

3 Big Shoe
Fashionable footwear for people with big feet! ◎ *Leliegracht 12 • Map L2*

4 SPRMRKT
Spacious and perpetually intriguing, this store is an absolute must for style aficionados who have a discerning eye for retro clothing and accessories, furniture and fabrics. ◎ *Rozengracht 191–193 • Map J3*

5 G.D.E. Jongejans
Vintage frames specialist selling a fascinating selection of eyewear dating from the 1800s onwards. If it's shut, just check out the window display. ◎ *Noorderkerkstraat 18 • Map D2*

6 Unlimited Delicious
Savour the signature hot chocolate, bonbons and sublimely flavoured pastries at this popular patisserie and chocolatier. Workshops are also on offer. ◎ *Haarlemmerstraat 122 • Map D2*

7 Kitsch Kitchen
A rainbow of colourful accessories for cooks and kitchens is on offer here. There is a good selection of fun kid's toys, including Mexican *piñatas*. ◎ *Rozengracht 8–12 • Map K3*

8 Mechanisch Speelgoed
A fascinating, nostalgia-inducing collection of mechanical toys and good old-fashioned children's playthings. Simply put: life before Xbox. (Closed Wed). ◎ *Westerstraat 67 • Map D2*

9 Pasta Panini
A fabulous Italian deli. Great for freshly-filled ciabattas at lunchtime or hand-made pasta for supper. Plus a tantalizing range of cookies, soup, sauces and wine. ◎ *Rozengracht 82 • Map K3*

10 papabubble
The caramel artisans in this store produce their unique, hand-crafted candy on site. Tahitian lime and bergamot are just some of the flavours used. ◎ *Haarlemmerdijk 70 • Map D1*

Left **GO Gallery** Right **Pancake Bakery**

Best of the Rest

1 The Movies
A fixture in Amsterdam, this art house cinema has been around since 1912 and is now also a restaurant and café. Shows international movies and independent productions. ✆ *Haarlemmerdijk 161-163 • Map D1*

2 Architectura & Natura
Bookshop and publisher specialising in architecture, gardening and natural history. Knowledgeable staff and a wide selection of English-language books. ✆ *Leliegracht 22 • Map L2*

3 't Geveltje
Beginners and pros jam together every Thursday night in the Jordaan's famous jazz bar for musicians and jazz aficionados alike. ✆ *Bloemgracht 170 • Map J2*

4 GO Gallery
Friendly neighbourhood gallery hosting shows with figurative and abstract art by international artists.
✆ *Prinsengracht 64 • Map L1*

5 Meeuwig & Zn.
Stockists of a prodigious range of olive oils selected from small farmers around the Mediterranean. Also sells vinegars, mustards and spices.
✆ *Haarlemmerstraat 70 • Map D2*

6 Two for Joy
This small, independent roasting company and café serves up some of the best coffee in town, roasted daily on the premises. Cakes, breakfast and lunch are available, as are various bags of beans to enjoy at home.
✆ *Haarlemmerdijk 182 • 020 221 9552*

7 Petticoat
Vintage clothing and accessories including a great selection of 1950s dresses and petticoats. There is also a growing collection of gothic clothing. ✆ *Lindengracht 99 • Map D2*

8 Pancake Bakery
Although unashamedly touristy, you could do a lot worse than this restaurant in a former 17th-century warehouse named "Hope". ✆ *Prinsengracht 191 • Map L1*

9 Paradox
A paradox in itself, this coffeeshop shows few traces of serving "the herb". Fresh fruit and veg shakes, healthy food and a bright interior make it a perfect place for breakfast or lunch.
✆ *Eerste Bloemdwarsstraat 2 • Map K2*

10 Small World
Simply the best quick-stop for sandwiches, carrot cake and other delicious offerings. ✆ *Binnen Oranjestraat 14 • Map D1*

Left **Vintage robots for sale at the Looier Kunst an Antiekcentrum** Right **Leidseplein at night**

Central Canal Ring

AMSTERDAM'S THREE GREAT CANALS, *Herengracht, Keizersgracht and Prinsengracht*, are at their most impressive in this central section of the *Grachtengordel (see p11)*, which culminates in the stretch known as the *Golden Bend*, where the wealthiest Amsterdammers built stately houses in the 1660s. Designed and decorated by the best architects of the day, such as Philips Vingboons, the mansions built here were often twice the width of standard canal houses. Nowadays, many of these buildings are occupied by institutions. In contrast, the intimate cross-streets that run between the three canals, known as De Negen Straatjes (The Nine Streets) enticingly display the city's talent for creative retail. Another magnet for shoppers is Metz & Co, which provides a bird's-eye view of the whole area from its top-floor café.

Cutting through this elegant district is the main thoroughfare, Leidsestraat, which culminates in the brash and lively entertainment hub, Leidseplein. Architectural highlights include the Paleis van Justitie and the American Hotel.

1891 turret, Metz & Co

Sights

1. Golden Bend
2. Bijbels Museum
3. Stadsarchief
4. Metz & Co
5. Leidsegracht
6. Negen Straatjes
7. Felix Meritis Building
8. Looier Kunst en Antiekcentrum
9. Leidseplein
10. American Hotel

Museum garden, Bijbels Museum

Golden Bend

So named because of the concentration of wealth amongst its first residents, this stretch of the Herengracht between Vijzelstraat and Leidsestraat feels grand but bland, unless you pick out eye-catching details as you stroll. Look out for Louis XIV-style No. 475, said to be Amsterdam's most beautiful house; and No. 476, elegantly restyled in the 1730s and topped with an eagle. No. 497 is open to the public, but you have to like cats: it's the Kattenkabinet, a unique museum devoted to cats in art. Be careful not to trip over one of the many feline attendants. *Kattenkabinet: Herengracht 497 • Map M6 • 020 626 9040 • www.kattenkabinet.nl • Open 10am–4pm Mon–Fri, noon–5pm Sat–Sun • Admission charge*

Bijbels Museum

Far lovelier than the Golden Bend is the stretch of Herengracht between Huidenstraat and Leidsestraat, particularly Nos 364–70, four houses built by Philips Vingboons in 1662. Two of them house the Bible Museum, where apart from biblical artifacts you can admire the early18th-century interior and take a stroll in the peaceful garden. *Herengracht 366–368 • Map L5 • 020 624 2436 • www.bijbelsmuseum.nl • Open 10am–5pm Mon–Sat, 11am–5pm Sun • Closed 1 Jan, 30 Apr • Admission charge*

Stadsarchief

The Stadsarchief, which houses the city's municipal archives, has moved from its old location in Amsteldijk and now occupies a monumental building designed by the Amsterdamse School architect De Bazel. It was completed in 1926 and is full of original features. One of the largest buildings in the city centre, it was originally the headquarters of the Netherlands Trading Corporation (now ABN Amro). *Vijzelstraat 32 • Map 4 F2 • Tram 16, 24, 25 • 020 251 1511 • www.stadsarchief.amsterdam.nl • Open 10am–5pm Tue–Fri, noon–5pm Sat–Sun • Closed public holidays*

Metz & Co

The great attraction of this ponderous late-19th century building (apart, of course, from the seven floors of luxury goods on sale) is its sixth-floor cupola and café, with superb views of the canal ring below. Originally built for an insurance company in 1891, it was taken over by Metz & Co in 1908. Gerrit Rietveld added his splendid glass cupola in 1930. In 1973, Liberty of London bought the business, renovated the building and commissioned Cees Dam to design the sixth-floor café. *Leidsestraat 34–36 • Map L6 • 020 520 7020 • Open 11am–6pm Mon, 9:30am–6pm Tue–Sat, noon–5pm Sun • www.metz-co.com*

The Stadsarchief

5 Leidsegracht

For dream canal houses in pristine condition, look no further than sophisticated Leidsegracht, one of the city's most sought-after addresses. At Herengracht 394, on the corner with Leidsegracht, notice the fine wall plaque depicting characters from a medieval legend – the four *Heemskinderen* on their horse Beyaart. Another plaque, at No. 39, shows Cornelis Lely, who drew up the original plans for draining the Zuiderzee. ◈ *Map K6*

6 Negen Straatjes

Nestling in the centre of the canal ring are these three parallel rows of cross-streets bordered by Singel and Prinsengracht to east and west, and Raadhuisstraat and Leidsegracht to north and south. Known collectively as the Nine Streets, these charming roads were once a centre for the leather trade. Today they are packed with amusing, imaginative and sometimes eccentric shops like De Witte Tandenwinkel, devoted to toothbrushes *(see p104)*. In Gasthuismolensteeg, don't miss the Brilmuseum at No. 7, an enchanting museum and shop devoted to spectacles old and new (open noon–5pm Wed–Sat). ◈ *Map L4*

Felix Meritis Building

7 Felix Meritis Building

The splendid Neo-Classical façade of this building comes as a surprise on gabled Keizersgracht. Designed in 1787 by Jacob Otten Husly as a science and arts centre (the name Felix Meritis means "happiness through merit"), it flourished until the late 19th century. Later, it became headquarters of the Dutch Communist Party (CPN), and in the 1970s was home to the avant-garde Shaffy Theatre Company. Today, it houses the European Centre for Arts, Culture and Science – its arts complex and Summer University *(see p143)* mean it is always humming. ◈ *Keizersgracht 324 • Map L4 • 020 623 1311 • www.felix.meritis.nl*

8 Looier Kunst en Antiekcentrum

If the smart shops of the Spiegelkwartier *(see p112)* are too expensive and rarified, try searching for more affordable antiques in this warren of stalls occupying a vast network of ground-floor rooms in a block of houses near the Looiersgracht (tanners' canal). Taken together, this is the largest collection of art and antiques in the Netherlands. The stall-holders have a lively community spirit, hosting bridge sessions which are open to all. ◈ *Elandsgracht 109 • Map J5 • Open 11am–5pm Sat–Thu • www.looier.com*

Houseboats

Around 2,500 houseboats are called "home" in Amsterdam, but it was only after World War II, when there was a severe housing shortage, that they became popular. They are linked to the city's electricity and water supplies and sewage is pumped into an onshore facility. Visit the Woonbootmuseum (Houseboat Museum) opposite Prinsengracht 296 to find out more.

Leidseplein

The city's tourist hub. Sophisticated it is not, tacky and fun (and, at night, often raucous) it is, especially in summer, when buskers and street performers, from family pop groups to lone fire-eaters, keep the milling throngs amused. Leidseplein is a natural gathering place, packed with fast food stalls, cafés and smoking coffeeshops. Nightspots De Melkweg, Paradiso, and Holland Casino are close at hand, while for a more reflective diversion you can play chess on a giant outdoor chessboard in adjacent Max Euweplein *(see p116)*, or find the hidden sculpture in the tiny Leidsebos park. ◈ *Map C5*

Amsterdam American Hotel

One of Leidseplein's landmarks is this one-off Dutch interpretation of Art Nouveau by Willem Kromhout (1902), which foretold the Amsterdam School of architecture. Only the exterior is of interest: the interior is as bland as any other chain hotel. The exception is the hotel's famous Café Americain, with its stained-glass windows and glass parasol lampshades. The literati who once inhabited it may have disappeared, but it's a welcome haven from the rigours of Leidseplein. ◈ *Leidsekade 97 • Map C5 • 020 556 3000*

The Amsterdam American Hotel

Exploring the Central Canal Ring

Morning

This compact area is focused on Amsterdam's most famous canals, so why not start the day with a canal tour. Amsterdam Canal Cruises start and end on Stadhouderskade, opposite the Heineken Brewery. From here, it's a short walk to **Leidseplein** and welcome refreshment at the **Café Americain**.

Leaving the hubbub of Leidseplein, walk along Prinsengracht (passing the Paleis van Justitie, once the city orphanage) to elegant **Leidsegracht**. If there's time, investigate the antiques market, **Looier**, in Elandsgracht. For lunch, try brown cafés Van Puffelen or Het Molenpad, or designer hang-out Walem *(see p102)*.

Afternoon

Plunge into the **Negen Straatjes** for some serious shopping in its frivolous shops. You may not be able to resist the cakes and chocolate on offer at Chocolaterie Pompadour *(see p104)*. Pop into the Houseboat Museum, moored on Prinsengracht opposite Elandsgracht, to marvel at how a bargeman and his family could have lived in such a tiny space. Then cross to Herengracht, which you will have seen earlier from the water, and stroll along, admiring its architectural gems around the **Bijbels Museum** and **Golden Bend** *(see p99)*. If it's before 6pm (5pm on Sun), end the afternoon with a bird's eye view of your day's exploration from the sixth-floor café at **Metz & Co** *(see p99)*.

Left **The Bar With No Name** Right **Van Puffelen**

Bars

De Admiraal
One of the smarter *proeflokalen* (tasting houses) in the city – and unlike the rest, De Admiraal closes late. Collapse on the couches after knocking back the liquors and *jenever*. ✆ *Herengracht 319 • Map L4 • 020 625 4334 • €€€*

The Bar With No Name
Known to the locals as Wolvenstraat 23, this 1970s-style lounge bar-restaurant is the haunt of young advertising darlings and other affluent beings. Open from breakfast to bedtime, it serves imaginative sandwiches, soup and pan-Asian cuisine. ✆ *Wolvenstraat 23 • Map L4 • 020 320 0843 • €€*

Café de Pels
A low-key, easygoing neighbourhood bar – locals read the papers at the big table by the window. A great place to recover from a hangover on a Sunday (breakfast is served until 1:30pm). ✆ *Huidenstraat 25 • Map L5*

Walem
One of the city's original designer bars, this was the creation of renowned Dutch architect, Gerrit Rietveld. Inside, it's bright and minimalist; outside, there are charming terraces. ✆ *Keizersgracht 449 • Map L6*

Lux
Split-level, late-opening designer bar. DJs spin every night. ✆ *Marnixstraat 403 • Map K6*

Het Molenpad
A charming brown bar near the Frozen Fountain (see p105) and the Leidsestraat – equally suitable for design lovers and the shopped-out. ✆ *Prinsengracht 653 • Map K5 • 020 625 9680 • €€*

Vyne
Wine bar-cum-Italian delicatessen with trademark interior by architect firm Concrete. ✆ *Prinsengracht 411 • Map K4*

Café Saarein
Once an infamous women-only bar, now men are welcome. Quiet during the week, rowdy at weekends. Pool table, good bar food. ✆ *Elandsstraat 119 • Map K4*

Van Puffelen
The rich and beautiful flock to this elegant haunt – the biggest brown bar in town. ✆ *Prinsengracht 377 • Map K3 • 020 624 6270 • €€*

De Zotte
This Belgian bar (appropriately named "Drunken Fool") has a huge range of beers. Delicious food helps soak it all up. ✆ *Raamstraat 29 • Map K6 • 020 626 8694 • €€*

Recommend your favourite bar on traveldk.com

Price Categories

For a three-course
meal for one with half
a bottle of wine (or
equivalent meal), taxes
and extra charges.

€ under €20
€€ €20–€30
€€€ €30–€45
€€€€ €45–€60
€€€€€ over €60

Los Pilones

TOP 10 Restaurants

1 Restaurant Vinkeles
Housed in the sumptuous Dylan Hotel *(see p144)*, this Michelin-starred restaurant is world famous for exciting, modern French cuisine. ⚲ *Keizersgracht 384 • Map L4 • 020 530 2010 • €€€€€*

2 Bojo
Inexpensive, informal and Indonesian – head here after most of the city's restaurants have gone to bed. ⚲ *Lange Leidsedwarsstraat 49–51 • Map D5 • 020 622 7434 • €*

3 Goodies
A culinary delight in the heart of the Nine Streets. Healthy soups, salads and sandwiches by day; the perfect pasta by night. ⚲ *Huidenstraat 9 • Map L5 • 020 625 6122 • €€*

4 Los Pilones
This Mexican cantina is small, but authentic. Savour the home cooking between slams of tequila. ⚲ *Kerkstraat 63 • Map L6 • 020 320 4651 • €€€*

5 Sumo
The Japanese interior is matched by an all-you-can-eat menu of sushi, hand rolls and curries. For the location, the price is very reasonable. ⚲ *Korte Leidsedwarsstraat 51 • Map K6 • 020 423 5131 • €€*

6 Balthazar's Keuken
Book ahead for this unique restaurant, which only serves a set three-course menu. ⚲ *Elandsgracht 108 • Map K4 • 020 420 2114 • Open Wed–Fri (by request Sat–Tue) • €€€*

7 Nomads
This late-night restaurant is the ultimate in decadent dining. Lounge on mattresses while food is served from bronze platters. DJs enhance the Arabian experience at weekends. ⚲ *Rozengracht 133 • Map J3 • 020 344 6401 • €€€€*

8 Rakang
Totally authentic Thai; one of the best of its kind in the city. Those in the know load up at their cheaper, equally delicious take-away next door. ⚲ *Elandsgracht 29–31 • Map K4 • 020 620 9551 • €€€*

9 Envy
This is one of Amsterdam's finest offerings. The chefs expertly combine flavours to create superb Mediterranean delicacies. ⚲ *Prinsengracht 381 • Map K4 • 020 344 6407 • €€€*

10 Wagamama
Fast food, slow service – but you could do worse for a quick lunch. Don't miss the king-size chess action taking place on the giant board outside. ⚲ *Max Euweplein 10 • Map C5 • 020 528 7778 • €€*

Left **Pontifex** Right **Skins Cosmetics**

Shopping (Nine Streets)

Bakkerij Paul Année
Where can you find the best bread in Amsterdam? At this organic baker's outlet, selling a delicious range of wholemeal bread and croissants, pizza, tofu *broodjes* and sugar-free oatcakes. ✪ *Runstraat 25 • Map K5*

Skins Cosmetics
An exclusive range of perfumes and cosmetics are on offer in this stark and laboratory-like shop. ✪ *Runstraat 9 • Map K5 • www.skins.nl*

De Kaaskamer
For cheese with a capital C, try "The Cheese Chamber", where there are over 200 different kinds of one of Holland's best exports. If it isn't here, it probably doesn't exist. ✪ *Runstraat 7 • Map K5*

Van Ravenstein
Exclusive boutique selling designer wear by Dutch, Belgian, French and English designers including Dries van Noten. ✪ *Keizersgracht 359 • Map L5*

Brilmuseum/ Brillenwinkel
This fascinating spectacles museum and shop, housed in a 1620 building, explores the history of glasses and sells vintage frames as well as contemporary models. ✪ *Gasthuismo-lensteeg 7 • Map L3*

Pontifex
This tiny waxworks gives Madame Tussauds a run for their money, with a colourful range of candles of every type imaginable. Adjoining are the premises of the rather spooky doll doctor, Kramer. ✪ *Reestraat 20 • Map K3*

Chocolaterie Pompadour
You can pile on the calories just staring at the window display of this chic chocolaterie. Try the famous home-made choco-lates or Pompadour's exquisite tarts. ✪ *Huidenstraat 12 • Map L5*

Fifties-Sixties
Iconic toasters, chrome ashtrays and lamps aplenty are just some of the retro gems from the 1950s and 1960s waiting to be discovered in this browsable shop. ✪ *Reestraat 5 • Map L3*

De Witte Tandenwinkel
A veritable ode to the tooth, this shop specializes in every shape or size of toothbrush imaginable, and is sure to take your (bad) breath away. Mouthy Mick Jagger has even dropped by. ✪ *Runstraat 5 • Map L5*

Zipper
Immaculately displayed vintage second-hand clothes and accessories. ✪ *Huidenstraat 7 • Map L5*

Left **Frozen Fountain** Right **Melkweg**

TOP 10 Best of the Rest

1 Bagels & Beans
American-style freshly-baked cookies and cheesecake, freshly-squeezed juices and decent-sized cups of coffee. ⊗ *Keizersgracht 504 • Map L5*

2 Ben & Jerry's
Treat your inner child to some seriously delicious ice cream. ⊗ *Leidsestraat 90 • Map K6*

3 Frozen Fountain
Arguably, Amsterdam's most important designer store and exhibition space for furniture and home accessories. A revered international reputation for its cutting-edge designs and fresh talent makes it a must-see. ⊗ *Prinsengracht 645 • Map K5*

4 Urban Home & Garden Tours
Garden designer André Ancion gives English-language walking tours delving behind the façades of some of the city's most impressive canal houses. ⊗ *062 168 1918 • www.uhgt.nl*

5 Melkweg
Known in the 1970s as an alternative cultural meeting place, today this former milk factory hosts live music events. Plus there's a cinema, theatre, café-bar, gallery, upstairs bar and video room *(see p57)*.

6 Paradiso
One of Amsterdam's best-loved live music spots. Velvet Underground and Macy Gray have played here. The upstairs hall often has unknowns before they go big. ⊗ *Weteringschanss 6-8 • Map C5 • 020 626 4521 • www.paradiso.nl*

7 Hotel Pulitzer
August, at this prestigious hotel, is the time when hampers and champagne come out in full force. A floating stage is set up out front for the unmissable Grachtenfestival's open-air classical concerts *(see p70)*. ⊗ *Prinsengracht 315–331 • Map K3*

8 Cortina Papier
A wonderful selection of beautiful, handbound books and albums, printed and marbled wrapping papers, and inks in all colours. ⊗ *Reestraat 22 • Map K3*

9 Raïnaraï
An utterly charming Algerian deli producing delicious, authentic dishes using spices imported from the North African country. Takeaway, but also a few seats inside. ⊗ *Prinsengracht 252 • Map K3*

10 Japan Inn
Small in size but big in popularity, this place serves excellent sushi. ⊗ *Leidsekruisstraat 4 • Map D5*

Left **Munttoren** Right **Shire horses at the Heineken Experience**

Eastern Canal Ring

BEGUN IN THE EARLY 17TH CENTURY, *the Grachtengordel (see p11) was extended further east to reach the Amstel in the 1660s, making new plots of land available for wealthy merchants to build their luxurious if sober town houses. Among the highlights of the area are two such patrician mansions, the Museum Van Loon and the Museum Willet-Holthuysen. Medieval Amsterdam is recalled at the Munttoren, whose base was once part of the Regulierspoort, a gate in the city wall; by contrast, you can see the modern city in full swing in lively Rembrandtplein, formerly a butter market.*

There are diverse opportunities for shopping among the antiques of the Spiegelkwartier, at the colourful Bloemenmarkt, and at vibrant Albert Cuypmarkt; or you could catch a movie at Abraham Tuschinski's extraordinary 1921 cinema, now lovingly restored and offering six screens. And to refresh the parts that other beers may or may not be able to reach, you can visit the original Heineken Brewery for a guided tour and a free beer.

Tuschinski Theatre

🔟 Sights

1	Museum Van Loon
2	Museum Willet-Holthuysen
3	Amstel River
4	Rembrandtplein
5	Tuschinski Theatre
6	Munttoren
7	Bloemenmarkt
8	Spiegelkwartier
9	Heineken Experience
10	Albert Cuypmarkt

Museum Van Loon

1 A chance to see inside a private canal house, whose grand yet approachable 18th-century interior recreates a bygone age *(see pp30–31)*.

Museum Willet-Holthuysen

2 Though it lacks the lived-in feel of the Museum Van Loon, this 17th-century canal house has its own special atmosphere. An air of stiff formality tinged with melancholy pervades its stately rooms: the Ballroom; the Blue Room, reserved for the men of the house, with painted ceiling by Jacob de Wit; the glittering Dining Room; and the delicate Garden Room, with views over the formal garden. The collections of its last owners, Louisa Holthuysen and her husband, Abraham Willet, are displayed throughout – paintings, glass, ceramics, silver. The top floor tells the story of the Willets and their art collection. It was the widowed Louisa who left the house and its contents to the city. She died a lonely death in 1885. ◈ *Herengracht 605 • Map P6 • Tram 4, 9, 14 • 020 523 1822 • www. willet-holthuysen.nl • Open 9am–5pm Mon–Fri, 11am–5pm Sat & Sun • Closed 1 Jan, 30 Apr, 25 Dec • Admission charge*

Museum Willet-Holthuysen

Magere Brug

Amstel River

3 No visit to Amsterdam is complete without a walk along the banks of the Amstel, the river whose mouth spawned a fishing settlement in the 12th century *(see p38)*. In 1222 the river was dammed, and Amsterdam turned from fishing to trade – the beginning of its expansion. Commercial barges still ply the river, passing Blauwbrug (Blue Bridge), inspired by the *belle époque* Pont Alexandre III in Paris, the much loved Magere Brug *(see p11)*, and the Amstelsluizen (sluice gates), which help to pump millions of gallons of fresh water into the canals to keep them from stagnating. ◈ *Map P5 • Tram 4, 7, 9, 10, 14*

Rembrandtplein

4 This former butter market has what you might call a split personality. In its centre is a 19th-century statue of Rembrandt set in a tranquil garden, but around its sides are neon-lit, low-brow and – at night – high-octane bars and cafés, packed with Amsterdammers and visitors alike. This is a great place for an early evening drink; you might choose grand cafés Schiller *(see p113)* and De Kroon *(see p50)*, as popular at the turn of the 20th century as they are now. ◈ *Map N6, P6 • Tram 4, 9, 14*

5 Tuschinski Theatre

Amsterdam's – perhaps the world's – most elaborate cinema was the extraordinary creation of a self-made Jewish tailor from Poland. Obsessed by film and the belief that it could change lives, he built this cinema in 1921. He was later to perish in Auschwitz, but his wonderful creation – termed Tuschinski Style for its unique mixture of influences – lives on. During an extensive, multi-million renovation, hitherto unknown paintings of Vogue-style ladies were uncovered and the theatre was returned to its former glory. Now a Pathé Cinema, much of the original charm remains. Be sure to buy a ticket for Screen One to admire the main theatre before the lights go down.
◈ Reguliersbreestraat 26–28 • Map N6 • Tram 4, 9, 14

6 Munttoren

Take a close look at the Mint Tower (it was briefly used as the city mint in 1673). Its bottom half is the remnant of a gate in the medieval city wall. When the gate burned down in 1618, Hendrick de Keyser slapped one of his clock towers (see p42) on top of the remains. The carillon of 1699 rings every 15 minutes.

Flower Power

The Dutch adore flowers, particularly tulips. They are everywhere, on window boxes, in houses, in shops and markets. You can buy bulbs at the Bloemenmarkt, visit the vast flower auction at Aalsmeer and the spring spectacle at Keukenhof (see p72-3), and cycle through the bulbfields near Leiden. But you won't find the mythical black tulip: it doesn't exist, though breeders are getting very close to it.

Blooms at the Bloemenmarkt

Today, there is a gift shop on the ground floor. ◈ Map N5 • Tram 4, 9, 14, 16, 24, 25

7 Bloemenmarkt

Undoubtedly one of Amsterdam's most picturesque sights, the flower market is a magnet for tourists. There are local shoppers too, buying armfuls for their houses, while visitors arrange for bulbs to be mailed home. Vendors once sailed up the Amstel from their nurseries to this spot on the Singel, selling their wares directly from their boats. Nowadays the stalls are still floating, though you wouldn't know it as they feel firmly fixed. ◈ Map M5, M6 • Tram 1, 2, 4, 5, 9, 14, 16, 24, 25

8 Spiegelkwartier

In the late 19th century, antique dealers with an eye for an opportunity began to set up shop on Nieuwe Spiegelstraat, leading to the Rijksmuseum. There are more than 80 specialist art and antique dealers in the area now, making it a sparkling, elegant place in which to stroll. Content yourself with looking longingly at the gleaming displays of antique furniture, porcelain and glass, or treat yourself to a faded old Delft tile for just a few euros from Kramer (see p112). ◈ Map D5 • Tram 1, 2, 5, 16, 24, 25

Heineken Experience

9 The biggest draw to Heineken's former brewery, which ceased production here in 1988, must be the free beer at the end of the tour (if you are over 18). Learn the story of Holland's most famous brewery, walk through the brewhouse with its huge copper stills, and visit the stables. Shire horses still deliver beer throughout the city (if only for publicity). Enjoy the mini-brewery and tasting bar. ◈ *Stadhouderskade 78 • Map D6 • Tram 7, 10, 16, 24, 25 • 020 523 9222 • www.heineken experience.com • Open 11am–5pm Mon–Sun. Closed 1 Jan, 30 Apr, 25 Dec, 26 Dec • Admission charge*

Albert Cuypmarkt

10 Shabby but vibrant, De Pijp is a district where a wide mix of immigrants, artists, students and young couples create a heady atmosphere. Albert Cuypmarkt, which has been trading since 1905, is its bustling hub. The street it occupies, once a canal, was named after Dutch landscape painter Albert Cuyp. With around 260 stalls, backed by all manner of shops and ethnic restaurants, its an unmissable experience. Typically Dutch food stalls – cheese, fish, waffles, – jostle merrily with clothes, fabrics, shoes and bags. ◈ *Albert Cuypstraat • Map D6 • Tram 4, 16, 24, 25 • www.albertcuyptmarkt.nl • Open 9am–5pm Mon–Sat*

Smoked fish in Albert Cuypmarkt

Exploring the Eastern Canal Ring

Morning

On a fine stretch of the **Amstel River**, dainty Magere Brug makes a good spot to begin. Walking north, follow the river's curve, pausing at Amstel 104 and its equally crooked neighbours. Reaching **Munttoren**, wander along the **Bloemenmarkt**, then head out to Reguliersbre-estraat to check out the incredible **Tuschinski Theatre** a little further along the street. Its Art Deco interior is worth visiting, even if you don't watch a film here.

Chic Utrechtsestraat, with its appealing selection of restaurants, cafés, delicatessens, boutiques and galleries, is perfect for both shopping and lunch. The best Indonesian *rijsttafel* in town is served at Tujuh Maret *(see p61)*.

Afternoon

From Utrechtsestraat cross to Amstelveld, where the wooden Amstelkerk lends a countrified air, and Reguliersgracht *(see p8)* intersects picturesquely with Prinsengracht. Make your way along Prinsengracht, cross Vijzelstraat, and dive into Weteringbuurt. On the other side of Prinsengracht, admire elegant Deutzenhofje (Nos 855–99), erected in 1695 for destitute women.

From here, it's only a short walk to the **Museum Van Loon** *(see pp30–31)*, or a little further to **Museum Willet-Holthuysen** *(see p107)*, after which you can wind down with a drink in jolly Rembrandtplein. Best cafés are Schiller *(see p113)* and De Kroon *(see p50)*.

Check out photography museum Foam at Keizersgracht 609.

Left **Mulligans** Right **Soho**

TOP 10 Bars

1 Het Dwarsliggertje
The name implies that this understated gay/mixed bar is the street's "sleeper". Indeed, in this street of loud and trendy gay clubs, it has the look and feel of a friendly local ❧ *Reguliersdwarsstraat 105 • Map N6 • www.hetdwarsliggertje.nl*

2 Café van Leeuwen
A beautiful Dutch corner café with a stunning canal view, just off the bustling Utrechtse-straat. ❧ *Keizersgracht 711 • Map E5 • 020 625 8215 • www.cafevanleeuwen.nl*

3 De Duivel
Cypress Hill and The Roots have joined the boisterous baggy brigade at Amsterdam's small but legendary hip hop bar. These days, the hip hop is melted down with anything from funk to disco. ❧ *Reguliersdwarsstraat 87 • Map N6*

4 De Huyschkaemer
A corner-located, split-level designer bar popular with a young arty crowd. Great atmosphere. ❧ *Utrechtsestraat 137 • Map E5 • 020 627 0575*

5 Helden
Knock back the cocktails while a DJ spins chillout music and upbeat house at this lounge bar-cum-restaurant serving international cuisine. ❧ *Eerste van der Helststraat 42 • Map D6 • 020 673 3332 • €€€*

6 Kingfisher
This large and modern bar is one of the best watering-holes in the Pijp. Offers imaginative Dutch and international cuisine. ❧ *Ferdinand Bolstraat 24 • Map D6 • 020 671 2395 • €*

7 Lellebel
Amsterdam's infamous – and only – dragshow bar, the complete antithesis of the testosterone-fuelled Rembrandt-plein nearby. At first glance it's unremarkable, but when Shirley Bassey is turned up on the soundsystem, the bar staff perform quite some routine. ❧ *Utrechtsestraat 4 • Map P6*

8 Mulligans
If you're tired of the Rembrandtplein, pop round the corner to this Irish bar for some good *craic*. ❧ *Amstel 100 • Map P6*

9 Café Krom
This 1950s-styled brown café is quickly becoming an Amsterdam tradition. The old jukebox pumps a stream of vinyl nostalgia. ❧ *Utrechtse-straat 76 • Map E5 • 020 624 5343*

10 Soho
The Soho has become the city's biggest pint- and punter-puller on this trendy gay street. ❧ *Reguliersdwarsstraat 36 • Map M6*

Price Categories

For a three course meal for one with half a bottle of wine (or equivalent meal), taxes and extra charges.	
€	under €20
€€	€20–€30
€€€	€30–€45
€€€€	€45–€60
€€€€€	over €60

Zushi

🔟 Restaurants

1 Pilsvogel
Tapas and candle light are the orders of the day in this cosy wooden bar and restaurant. Stop in for lunch while shopping at the nearby Albert Cuypmarkt, or for a long dinner accompanied by some local beers. ✎ *Gerard Douplein 14 • Map D6 • 020 664 6483 • €€€*

2 The Golden Temple
Vegetarian restaurant run by American Sikhs offering a range of Indian, Middle Eastern and Italian food with a homecooked feel. ✎ *Utrechtsestraat 26 • Map E5 • 020 626 8560 • €*

3 De Waaghals
This restaurant serves organic vegetarian food as well as locally-brewed organic wine and beer. ✎ *Frans Halsstraat 29 • Map D6 • 020 679 9609 • €€€*

4 Bazar
Cheap and flavourful North African cuisine in the heart of Amsterdam's largest outdoor market, Albert Cuypmarkt *(see p61 & p109)*. ✎ *Albert Cuypstraat 182 • Map E6 • 020 779 7450 • €€*

5 Greetje
Enjoy traditional French cuisine, Dutch classics and Oude Jenever *(see p59)* in this cosy restaurant. ✎ *Peperstraat 23-25 • Map R3 • 020 779 7450 • €€€€*

6 Rose's Cantina
This Mexican cantina has Tex-Mex down to a tee – the food is varied and delicious, and the margaritas are served in pitchers! ✎ *Reguliersdwarsstraat 38 • Map M6 • 020 625 9797 • €€€*

7 Bouchon du Centre
Hanneke cooks fresh produce she's bought from the markets that day, and serves you from her open kitchen. One of the city's best-kept secrets. ✎ *Falckstraat 3 • Map E5 • 020 330 1128 • €€€*

8 Utrechtsedwarstafel
Pick a number of courses, choose a range from simple to gastronomic, and leave the rest to the wine connoisseur and cook duo who run this unusual eaterie. ✎ *Utrechtsedwarsstraat 107-109 • Map E5 • 020 625 4189 • €€€€*

9 Beddington's
The menu at Jean Beddington's restaurant is truly international, offering exciting dishes with hints of Japan, the Mediterranean and England. ✎ *Utrechtsestraat 141 • Map E5 • 020 620 7393 • €€€€*

10 Zushi
Hyper-modern and hyped-up, this is the place to be if you like your sushi with a zing. ✎ *Amstel 20 • Map P6 • 020 330 6882 • €€*

Left **Tóth-Ikonen** Right **Aalderink Oriental Art**

Antique Shops

1 Aalderink Oriental Art
Aalderink is the oldest and most reputable dealer of Asian Art and Ethnographics in the Netherlands, specializing in fine Japanese *netsuke* and *okimono*.
Ⓝ *Spiegelgracht 15 • Map D5*

2 Aronson Antiquairs
David Aronson opened this prestigious gallery around 1900; now it is run by his great-great-grandson. Early Delftware, continental 17th-and 18th-century furniture, plus Chinese *famille verte* and *famille rose* porcelain – much of it rare.
Ⓝ *Nieuwe Spiegelstraat 39 • Map D5*

3 E H Ariëns Kappers / C P J van der Peet BV
A huge range of mid-16th-to mid-20th-century prints, including a remarkable selection of Japanese woodblock prints.
Ⓝ *Prinsengracht 677 • Map D5*

4 Staetshuys Antiquairs
A curiosity shop selling odd scientific instruments, globes and other unusual objects.
Ⓝ *Nieuwe Spiegelstraat 45A • Map D5*

5 Frans Leidelmeijer
Frans Leidelmeijer, knighted for his services to the arts, runs this tasteful decorative arts shop.
Ⓝ *Lijnbaansgracht 369H • Map D5*

6 Eduard Kramer
Decorative Dutch tiles, Blue Delftware, antique books, prints, pewter, candlesticks and lamps.
Ⓝ *Nieuwe Spiegelstraat 64 • Map D5*

7 Thom & Lenny Nelis
A fascinating and unusual collection of medical instruments dating from the early 18th to the early 20th century. Ⓝ *Keizersgracht 541 • Map M6*

8 Tóth-Ikonen
The only icon specialist in the Spiegelkwartier, and the oldest in Amsterdam. Behold a dazzling array of 16th-to 19th-century Russian icons – including a large collection of brass travelling icons.
Ⓝ *Nieuwe Spiegelstraat 68 • Map D5*

9 Marjan Sterk
An exquisite selection of antique, Art Deco and Art Nouveau jewellery, plus 18th-and 19th-century Dutch silver. Open by appointment only.
Ⓝ *Nieuwe Spiegelstraat 63 • Map D5*

10 Van Dreven Antiquair
Alive with the sound of ticking, this shop proffers an eclectic selection of clocks from the early 17th century to the 1930s, plus a treasured collection of music boxes.
Ⓝ *Nieuwe Spiegelstraat 38 • Map D5*

Left **NH Schiller** Right **Bloemenmarkt**

TOP 10 Best of the Rest

1 Museum of Bags and Purses

This unique museum illustrates the history of the western handbag, dating from the late middle ages right up to the present. Over 4,000 bags, purses, suitcases and pouches are on display. ⊗ *Herengracht 573 • Map E4 • 020 524 6452 • www.tassenmuseum.nl*

2 Bloemenmarkt

The legendary floating flower market *(see p108)*.

3 Concerto

Simply the best record store in town; new and secondhand. ⊗ *Utrechtsestraat 52 • Map E5*

4 Soup en Zo

This one-stop modern soup kitchen is just a short walk from the Rijksmuseum. Great for takeaways, but some seats are available. Over half the soups are vegetarian. ⊗ *Nieuwe Spiegelstraat 54 • Map D5*

5 Hemp Hotel

Little escapes being hemp-ified at this small, family-run hotel – from the hemp futons to the fresh hemp muffins served at breakfast, and the hemp beer served in the late-opening Hemple Temple Nightbar. ⊗ *Frederiksplein 15 • Map E5 • 020 625 4425*

6 Heineken Experience

If you're here for the beer, this self-guided tour of the original Heineken brewery is a must. Entrance includes three glasses of the famous brew *(see p109)*.

7 Magere Brug

The city's best-known bridge – worth a wander for perfect photo opportunites, the stunning views, or simply to watch the drawbridge in action. Romantic at night when it's all lit up *(see p11)*.

8 The Otherside

For a perfectly pink joint, head to this gay friendly coffeeshop – a bright, modern, friendly place. ⊗ *Reguliersdwarsstraat 6 • Map M6*

9 NH Schiller

The hotel's brasserie is a gorgeous Art Nouveau escape from touristic Rembrandtplein. Owned for the best part of the last century by painter Frits Schiller, it was a regular meeting place for artists, and still has something of that atmosphere. Schiller's paintings are displayed throughout the premises *(see p146)*.

10 Village Bagels

Delicious bagels and fresh juices are served at this New York-style bagel shop. ⊗ *Vijzelstraat 137 • Map D5*

Left **Concertgebouw** Right **Max Euweplein**

Museum Quarter

UNTIL THE LATE 19TH CENTURY, *the Museum Quarter lay outside the city limits, a region of small farms and market gardens. Then the city council designated it an area of art and culture, and plans were conceived for the first of Amsterdam's celebrated cultural institutions. With its great museums of art, an internationally renowned concert hall, the city's largest park and a clutch of exclusive shopping streets, the Museum Quarter is today one of Amsterdam's most impressive areas.*

TOP 10 Sights

1. Rijksmuseum
2. Van Gogh Museum
3. Stedelijk Museum
4. Concertgebouw
5. Vondelpark
6. Coster Diamonds
7. Museumplein
8. Max Euweplein
9. De Hollandsche Manege
10. P C Hooftstraat

Rijksmuseum

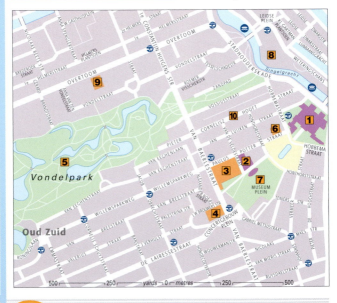

1 Rijksmuseum
Established by King Louis Napoleon in 1808 along the lines of the Paris Louvre, the Rijksmuseum collection has grown in the intervening years to nearly seven million works of art. It has moved twice since its beginnings in the Royal Palace on the Dam. Since 1885 it has been housed in P J H Cuypers' ornate Neo-Gothic building *(see pp12–15).*

2 Van Gogh Museum
The uncompromisingly modern building by De Stijl architect Gerrit Rietveld was specially designed to display the nation's collection of this disturbed yet brilliant artist's work *(see pp16–19).*

3 Stedelijk Museum
Devoted to modern art and design from the mid-19th century to the present day, this museum has an impressive collection. The stunning additional wing has increased the exhibition area so more artworks can be shown, as well as space for a café and shop *(see p40).* ◈ *Museumplein 10 • Map C6 • Tram 2, 3, 5, 12 • 020 573 2911 • www.stedelijk.nl*

4 Concertgebouw
One of the world's great concert halls, the Concertgebouw was built in 1888, designed by A L Van Gendt in Neo-Dutch Renaissance style with a colonnaded neo-Classical façade. In the 1980s, the building was discovered to be in danger of collapse. In time for the centenary of both the concert hall and its world-famous orchestra, new foundations were laid, and the building was restored and enlarged. Amazingly, all this took place without it having to close. ◈ *Concertgebouwplein 10 • Map C6 • Tram 2, 3, 5, 12, 16, 24 • 020 573 0573 • www.concertgebouw.nl • Box office open 1–5pm daily*

5 Vondelpark
Founded in 1864 by a group of philanthropic citizens, this congenial park was later named after the 17th-century poet Joost van den Vondel. Landscaped on informal English lines in 1865 – and enlarged in 1877 – by father and son J D and L P Zocher, with wide green vistas, a profusion of trees and lakes, a rose garden and a bandstand, it became a mecca for hippies in the late 1960s and 1970s. It is still a lively place on summer days, when people flock to hear concerts and plays in the open-air theatre *(see p71),* glimpse the occasional juggler or fire-eater, jog, rollerblade or play football. There are many different species of plants, trees and wildlife. A distinctive landmark, looking a little like a neat boater turned upside-down, is the round Blauwe Theehuis (Blue Teahouse), built by H A J Baanders in 1936 in the New Functionalist style *(see p50).* ◈ *Stadhouderskade • Map A6 • Tram 1, 2, 3, 5, 12*

Bandstand in Vondelpark

Diamonds

Amsterdam has been a centre of diamond cutting, polishing and trading since the 16th century, when Jews, fleeing the Spanish Inquisition, brought the business to the city. The trade flourished in the late 19th century with the influx of Jews from Antwerp, many of them skilled in the industry, and with the import of diamonds from South Africa.

6 Coster Diamonds

Founded in 1840 and now occupying three grand villas, Coster is one of a handful of diamond workshops offering free guided tours. These 30-minute tours give you the opportunity to observe stone graders, cutters and polishers at work. In 1852, the *Koh-i-Noor* (mountain of light) diamond was re-polished here for the British Crown Jewels, and a replica of the crown that contains it – incorporating a copy of the fabulous blue-white stone – is displayed in the entrance hall. There are diamonds and jewellery for sale here as well as at the Diamond Museum next door. ◈ *PaulusPotterstraat 2–8*
• *Map C5* • *Tram 2, 5* • *020 305 5555*
• *www.costerdiamonds.com*
• *Open 9am–5pm daily* • *Free*

Coster Diamonds

7 Museumplein

The city's largest square was first landscaped in 1872, but it was ruined in 1953 when a hair-raising stretch of road – which locals nicknamed "the shortest motorway in Europe" – was built across it. Completely redesigned between 1990 and 1996, it is now a great swathe of green, still more functional than beautiful, but giving an uninterrupted view from the Rijksmuseum to the Concert-gebouw. It has children's play areas and a pond that is frozen over to form an ice-rink in winter. Various events are staged here – from circuses to political demonstrations – and it is the setting for *Hel van Vuur* (Hell of Fire), a monument to all gypsies persecuted by the Nazis, as well as the Ravensbrück Memorial *(see p49)*. The district is one of the wealthiest in Amsterdam, with broad streets lined by grand houses. ◈ *Map C6* • *Tram 2, 3, 5, 12, 16, 24*

8 Max Euweplein

Named after the Netherlands only chess champion, Max Euwe (1901–81), this square is built on the site of the notorious World War II Huis van Bewaring (House of Detention). It is believed Anne Frank and her family were initially held here after their betrayal. A blue memorial with glass teardrops commemorates this dark passage of history. Nowadays, Max Euweplein has a livelier vibe, with the Hard Rock Café, Comedy Café and Holland Casino all located here. Chess buffs can visit the Max Euwe-Centrum (Chess Museum) or partake in a game on the oversized board in the square. Don't miss the pillared Neo-Classical façade of the Wetering-schans street entrance and its frieze. ◈ *Map C5* • *Tram 1, 2, 5, 7*

De Hollandsche Manege

9 De Hollandsche Manege

Magnificent and quite unexpected, concealed behind an unexceptional façade, A L van Gendt's Hollandsche Manege is a vast Neo-Classical indoor riding school, built in 1881. (It was commissioned to replace the original Dutch Riding School building, which was situated on Leidsegracht.) Based on the Spanish Riding School in Vienna, it sports elegant plasterwork, sculpted horses' heads, and a stunning open ironwork roof rising high above the sand arena. The school was threatened with demolition in the 1980s but public outcry saved it. If there is a lesson in progress, you can stay and watch. There is also a decent café. ⬿ Vondelstraat 140
• Map B5 • Tram 1 • 020 618 0942
• Open 10am–5pm Mon–Sun
• Admission charge

10 P C Hooftstraat

This elegant shopping street is to Amsterdam what Bond Street is to London. All the names in international fashion are here – Tommy Hilfiger, Hugo Boss, DKNY, Gucci, Mulberry, Emporio Armani – although well-heeled locals tend to favour friendlier Cornelis Schuytstraat nearby. ⬿ Map C5 • Tram 1, 2, 3, 5, 12

A Day in the Museum Quarter

Morning

Depending on your taste in art, start the day either in the **Rijksmuseum** *(see pp12–15)* or the **Van Gogh Museum** *(see pp16–19)*. If you choose the former, be selective as the collection is extensive and is spread over three floors of the museum *(see p12)*. Whichever museum you visit, you should aim to spend the whole morning there. The Van Gogh Museum has a useful ground floor café, and you can end your visit with a browse in the museum shop next to the main entrance.

Next, cross **Museumplein** to the **Concertgebouw** *(see p115)* and pop in for a look. Make your way to Art Deco Brasserie van Baerle (Van Baerlestraat 158) for lunch. It has a lovely shady garden and is popular, so it's worth booking a table.

Afternoon

Head back to Paulus Potterstraat and **Coster Diamonds**, where you could take one of the half-hour tours. Afterwards, walk along Hobbemastraat until you reach the elegant shops of **P C Hooftstraat**. Turn left and window-shop your way along the street.

If your feet are up to it, spend an hour or so strolling around the Vondelpark, finishing either at the Blauwe Theehuis *(see p50)* or the **Filmmuseum's** Café Vertigo, which has a lovely terrace overlooking the park. You could end with a visit to the **De Hollandsche Manege**, which opens till midnight on weekdays.

Price Categories

For a three-course	€ under €20
meal for one with half	€€ €20–€30
a bottle of wine (or	€€€ €30–€45
equivalent meal), taxes	€€€€ €45–€60
and extra charges.	€€€€€ over €60

The College Hotel

Food and Drink

1 De Bakkerswinkel
This bakery with seats inside is an ideal spot for breakfast, lunch or high tea – but beware, it can get crowded. ✆ *Roelof Hartstraat 68 • 020 662 3594*

2 The College Hotel
This elegant restaurant serves classic Dutch dishes with a contemporary twist. ✆ *Roelof Hartstraat 1 • 020 571 1511 • €€€€*

3 Brasserie van Baerle
This polished contemporary brasserie is popular with Dutch celebs for its well-reputed wine list, and imaginative French cuisine. ✆ *Van Baerlestraat 158 • Map C6 • 020 679 1532 • €€€€*

4 Cobra Café
Wine and dine at this designer café on Museumplein created as an ode to the members of the CoBrA art movement. The stylish bar serves delicious cocktails and snacks. ✆ *Museumplein • Map C6 • 020 470 0111 • €€*

5 Simple Bar
This fashionable bar is popular with 30-somethings. ✆ *Overtoom 50 • Map C5*

6 Le Garage
The famous and beautiful of Amsterdam fill their tummies and empty their wallets here. The food is a delicate fusion of French with international cuisine. ✆ *Ruysdaelstraat 54–56 • Map C6 • 020 679 7176 • €€€€*

7 Momo
This Asian-inspired restaurant and lounge is big with the suit-and-tie crowd. An extensive cocktail menu completes the experience. ✆ *Hobbemastraat 1 • Map C5 • 020 671 7474 • €€€€*

8 Boutique Restaurant Maxime
This chic brasserie is the perfect pit stop during a shopping trip down PC Hooftstraat. Come the evening it transforms into a romantic French restaurant. ✆ *PC Hooftstraat 63 • Map C5 • 020 676 5306*

9 Café Toussaint
This charming, relaxed café-bar has an open kitchen serving delicious lunches and dinners. ✆ *Bosboom Toussaintstraat 26 • Map J6 • 020 685 0737 • €€€*

10 Café Wildschut
Boasting an extensive menu, Art Deco interior and a sheltered, south-facing terrace, Café Wildschut has something for everyone. ✆ *Roelof Hartplein 1–3 • 020 676 8220*

Recommend your favourite café on traveldk.com

Left **De Hollandsche Manege** Right **De Peperwortel**

TOP 10 Best of the Rest

1 Brasserie Maxie's
Step downstairs into this cosy café, open seven days a week. Warm yourself by the fire in winter or simply enjoy the varied, international menu. *PC Hooftstraat 100 • Map C5 • 020 679 2004*

2 Het Blauwe Theehuis
This teahouse in the Vondelpark is one of the city's best-kept secrets, despite its central location. *Vondelpark 5 • Map B6 • 020 662 0254*

3 Broekmans & Van Poppel
Founded in 1914, this store has one of the largest collections of sheet music in the world. *Van Baerlestraat 92–94 • Map C6*

4 Concertgebouw
Every Wednesday at 12:30pm (except in summer) there are free lunchtime concerts here. Informal atmosphere, unsurpassed quality; queue early *(see p115)*.

5 Marqt
Fresh food sourced from local suppliers and independent producers are to be found at this hip organic store. *Overtoom 21 • Map C5 • 020 422 6311*

6 Friday Night Skate
Join this huge group of skaters for a free, 2-hour, 20 km (12 mile) tour of the city. Any competent skater can join in. Gather from 8pm. *Vondelpark (Roemer Visscherstraat entrance) • Map C5 • www.fridaynightskate.com*

7 De Hollandsche Manege
One of the more unusual places to stop for a drink in town. The upstairs café of this stables overlooks the sand arena below as classes are being held *(see p117)*.

8 De Peperwortel
This charming *traiteur* is ideally placed for picnicking in the park. Delicious quiches, pasta, salads and soup, with vegetarians particularly well catered for. Plus a choice selection of wine. *Overtoom 140 • Map B5 • 020 685 1053*

9 Vondelpark Openluchttheater
Catch a bit of drama, flamenco, puppetry or pop in the Vondelpark's open-air theatre *(see p71)*. *Vondelpark • Map B6 • Jun–Aug: Fri–Sun*

10 Zuiderbad
This restored Art Nouveau swimming pool, dating from 1911, is the city's most stylish place to bathe. *Hobbemastraat 26 • Map D6*

For more information on the Friday Night Skate, visit www.fridaynightskate.com

Left **Koninklijk Theater Carré** Right **Werfmuseum 't Kromhout**

Plantage

VISITORS FLOCK TO AMSTERDAM'S EXCELLENT ZOO, *but the rest of this distinguished residential district, with its elegant villas and broad, tree-lined streets, is often overlooked. Most of the villas appeared in the 19th century, many of them occupied by Jews who had prospered in the diamond industry, and the neighbourhood's strong Jewish tradition is reflected in its numerous memorials. Plantage means plantation: this was a rural area until the final extension of the Grachtengordel in 1638. Despite its tranquillity, there is no shortage of places to visit and sights to see.*

🔟 Sights

1. Het Scheepvaartmuseum
2. Artis Royal Zoo
3. Tropenmuseum
4. Werfmuseum 't Kromhout
5. Verzetsmuseum
6. Hortus Botanicus
7. De Burcht
8. Hollandsche Schouwburg
9. Koninklijk Theater Carré
10. Hermitage

Tropenmuseum sculpture

Previous pages **Bunches of brightly-coloured tulips on sale**

1 Het Scheepvaartmuseum

For anyone who loves ships, the maritime museum is a must. Where sails, ropes and guns were once stored is now an Aladdin's Cave of nautical treasures *(see p41 and p68)*. All ages are catered for, with virtual adventures at sea and interactive shows for kids and adults alike. The restaurant and courtyard are open to everyone, not just those visiting the museum. ◉ *Kattenburgerplein 1 • Map G3 • 020 523 2222 • www.scheepvaartmuseum.nl • Call ahead for opening times • Open Sep–May: 10am–5pm Tue–Sun; Jun–Aug: daily; also open 10am–5pm Mon during school holidays. Closed 1 Jan, 30 Apr, 25 Dec • Admission charge*

2 Artis Royal Zoo

If you want to give human culture a break, the zoological garden makes a terrific contrast. About 900 species are kept in reasonably naturalistic surroundings, including an African landscape. Watch the Japanese monkeys grooming one another, the reptiles slithering in their steamy jungle or the only giant anteaters in Holland snuffling for prey. There are plenty of places where you can shelter from the rain, including the Planetarium, Geological and Zoological museums, and the Aquarium, home to more than 2,000 mesmerizing fish. ◉ *Plantage Kerklaan 38–40 • Tram 9, 14 • Map G4 • 0900 278 4796 • www.artis.nl • Open Apr–Oct: 9am–6pm daily (till sunset Jul–Aug); Nov–Mar: 9am–5pm daily • Guided tour 11am Sat & Sun • Admission charge*

3 Tropenmuseum

Originally built to celebrate Dutch colonialism, visitors to the Tropenmuseum will find unusual objects from around the world. Set in one of the city's finest historic buildings, the museum mixes ethnography with popular and contemporary art. The separate Tropenmuseum Junior is strictly for 6–13 year olds (no adults unless accompanied by a child). ◉ *Linnaeusstraat 2 • Tram 9, 10, 14; bus 22 • Map G5 • 020 568 8200 • www.tropenmuseum.nl • Open 10am–5pm Tue–Sun • Admission charge*

4 Werfmuseum 't Kromhout

In the 18th century, the Eastern docklands were packed with shipyards. Today this restored working yard is one of the few remaining. It has survived by moving with the times – concentrating on restoration when shipbuilding declined, producing the diesel engine that powered most inland waterways craft, and doubling as a museum. Its displays include tools, machinery, steam engines, photographs and an exhibition on 300 years of shipbuilding in the area. ◉ *Hoogte Kadijk 147 • Tram 9, 14; bus 22, 32 • Map G4 • 020 627 6777 • www.machinekamer.nl • Open 10am–3pm Tue • Groups by appointment only • Admission charge*

Artis Planetarium

The Dutch East India Company (VOC)

Amsterdam's wealth in the 17th century was in no small measure due to the success of the VOC. Founded in 1602, it had a trading monopoly east of the Cape of Good Hope. Its legendary fleet of "East Indiamen" *(see p68)* carried much of Europe's spice imports until it folded in 1791.

De Burcht

Verzetsmuseum

Following the development of the Dutch Resistance movement from the German invasion in May 1940 to the liberation in May 1945, this exhibition shows how the Dutch people courageously faced the occupation. Its fascinating and evocative displays relate private stories of individual heroism and place them in their historical context. Among the memorabilia are forged identity papers, old photographs and underground newspapers. ⊗ *Plantage Kerklaan 61 • Map G4 • Tram 9, 14 • 020 620 2535 • www.verzetsmuseum.org • Open 10am–5pm Tue–Fri, 11am–5pm Sat–Mon • Closed 1 Jan, 30 Apr, 25 Dec • Admission charge*

Hortus Botanicus

About 4,000 different species of plants, flowers and trees, rock and herb gardens and numerous

Hortus Botanicus

glasshouses are crammed into this small botanical garden. Most of the exotic plants were collected by the VOC in the 17th and 18th centuries. Highlights are a 300-year old Cycad palm, the three-climates glasshouse and a coffee plant, Europe's first, smuggled out of Ethiopia in 1706. There is a lovely café here. ⊗ *Plantage Middenlaan 2A • Map R5 • Tram 9, 14 • 020 625 9021 • www.dehortus.nl • Open Feb–Nov: 9am–5pm Mon–Fri, 10am–5pm Sat, Sun & public holidays (Jul–Aug: until 7pm daily); Dec–Jan: 9am–4pm Mon–Fri, 10am–4pm Sat, Sun & public holidays • Closed 1 Jan, 25 Dec • Admission charge*

De Burcht (Vakbondsmuseum)

Nicknamed "the castle" because of its crenellated façade, this is the oldest Trades Union building in the Netherlands, built in 1899 by H P Berlage of Beurs fame *(see p84)* for the General Dutch Diamond Workers' Union (ANDB). Now fully restored, tours are available of the interior, from the stunning tiled entrance to the hand-carved staircase and wall murals. ⊗ *Henri Polaklaan 9 • Map F4 • Tram 9, 14 • 020 624 1166 • www.deburcht.org • Guided tours only; call for details • Admission charge*

Hollandsche Schouwburg

8 During the Nazi occupation, this former theatre was used as an assembly-point for thousands of Jews. Behind an intact façade, a garden has been created around a basalt monument on the site of the auditorium. Family names of 6,700 Dutch Jews are engraved in a memorial hall to the 104,000 who were exterminated. There is an exhibition upstairs. ✪ *Plantage Middenlaan 24 • Map F4 • Tram 9, 14 • 020 531 0340 • www.hollandscheschouwburg.nl • Open 11am–4pm daily • Closed Yom Kippur, Rosh Hashanah • Free*

Koninklijk Theater Carré

9 It is hard to believe that the magnificent Carré Theatre, superbly set beside the Amstel, was built at break-neck speed in 1887 to house Oscar Carré's circus. A copy of his other circus in Cologne, it has a fine Neo-Renaissance frontage, some splendid ironwork, and is decorated appropriately with the heads of clowns and dancers. Today, it hosts theatre and dance shows, musicals, and even the occasional circus. ✪ *Amstel 115–25 • Map F5 • Tram 7, 9, 10, 14 • 0900 252 5255 • www.carre.nl • Box office open 10am–8pm daily • Guided tours 11am Sat*

Hermitage

10 This building, formerly a home for elderly women, now houses the Hermitage museum showcasing Russian history and Dutch culture. A study centre, complete with computers and touchscreens, is also available for visitors to brush up on their knowledge of the Russian and Dutch Hermitage collections. ✪ *Amstel 51 • Map Q6 • Tram 4, 9, 14 • 020 530 7488 • www.hermitage.nl • Open 10am–5pm daily (to 8pm Wed) • Closed 1 Jan, 25 Dec • Admission charge*

A Day in the Plantage

Morning

🕐 Start your day among the cannons, models, figureheads, maps and instruments of the **Het Scheepvaartmuseum** *(see p123)*, then revive yourself at the pleasant ground-floor café. If you secretly hanker after a shipin-a-bottle, a cutlass paper knife or other objects with a nautical theme, visit the museum shop before you leave. Outside, take a look around the Amsterdam, the full-size replica of an 18thcentury East Indiaman.

If it is a Tuesday and you haven't yet had your fill of boats, take a short detour to the **Werf 't Kromhout Museum** *(see p123)* to see some shipbuilding in progress or, at the very least, the exhibition about it. Lunch at one of the cafés in Entrepotdok – such as Café 't Kromhout at No. 36.

Afternoon

After lunch, you could make your way to Plantage Kerklaan and the **Verzetsmuseum** *(see facing page)*. A visit here is definitely worthwhile, if harrowing. Afterwards, blow the cobwebs away by spending an hour or two at **Artis** *(see p123)*. For a few euros, the excellent zoo plan gives you feeding times, as well as pinpointing the two museums and the Aquarium. Head back towards the main entrance, where there is a café, and a shop selling goods with a wildlife theme. If there is time, you could finish your explorations with a quick dash around the solar system at the Planetarium.

Left **De Rieker Windmill, Amstelpark** Right **Ouderkerk aan de Amstel**

Further Afield

ENTRAL AMSTERDAM HAS MORE THAN ENOUGH *to keep any visitor occupied, but if time permits, it's certainly worth taking the trouble to explore the outskirts, where a diverse selection of sights is on offer. Football fans will want to make a beeline for the city's stunning stadium, Amsterdam ArenA, home of legendary soccer club Ajax. There are fascinating exhibits on view at the Cobra Museum, or hop over the IJ to the EYE Film Institute. If you are interested in architecture, make sure that you see the innovative 1920s buildings of the De Dageraad housing estate. If it's peace and quiet you want, there are several choices, including the small, historic town of Ouderkerk aan de Amstel – older than Amsterdam itself – and the wide open spaces of Amsterdamse Bos. The city's excellent transport system makes all these sights easily accessible, and some of them are not far from the centre – or from each other.*

🔟 Sights

1. Eye Film Institute
2. De Dageraad Housing
3. Amstelpark
4. Ajax Museum
5. Ouderkerk aan de Amstel
6. Amsterdamse Bos
7. Cobra Museum
8. Eastern Docklands
9. NEMO
10. Frankendael

De Dageraad Housing

EYE Film Insitute

EYE Film Institute

The EYE Film Institute Netherlands (previously the Filmmuseum) moved from the Vondelpark to the north bank of the River IJ, opposite Centraal Station, in 2012. Designed by Delugan Meissl Associated Architects, this impressive building consolidates a 1,200-square-metre (1292-square-foot) exhibition space; four cinemas; an interactive basement showcasing EYE's rich digital collection, with presentations about film history; and installations for children. There's also a well-stocked museum store and café with south-facing terrace. ⊗ *IJpromenade 1 • GVB Ferry "Buiksloterweg" (departs from behind Centraal Station) • 020 589 1400 • www.eyefilm.nl • Open 10–1am Sun–Thu; 10–2am Fri & Sat • Admission charge*

De Dageraad Housing

A housing estate seems an unlikely tourist attraction, but the complex built for the De Dageraad (Dawn) housing association from 1918–23 is well worth a visit – especially for anyone interested in the Amsterdam School of Architecture. Piet Kramer and Michel de Klerk designed sculptural buildings of great originality, with tiled roofs that undulate in waves, and brick walls that billow and curve. The project was part of an initiative to provide better housing for poorer families, in the wake of the revolutionary Housing Act of 1901. ⊗ *Pieter Lodewijk Takstraat • Tram 4,12,25*

Amstelpark

This welcome green space to the south of the city has a rose garden, a maze and an art gallery, as well as pony rides, farm animals and a miniature steam train for children. At its southern-most tip is the well-preserved De Rieker windmill. Built in 1636, it was a favourite of Rembrandt, whose statue stands nearby, and is now a private home. ⊗ *Europa-boulevard • Metro RAI; Tram 4; Bus 66, 199 • Open dawn–dusk*

Ajax Museum

Football fans will want to pay their respects to the brilliant Ajax club at their impressive stadium, Amsterdam ArenA. Visit the interactive museum, which brings the club and its greatest moments to life, and tour the state-of-the-art 50,000-seat stadium. There are usually six tours a day in summer, four in winter, except on event days; phone ahead for times. ⊗ *Arena Boulevard 1 • Metro to Strandvliet or Bijlmer; train to Bijlmer • 020 311 1333/ 020 311 1336 • www.amsterdamarena.nl • Open Apr–Sep: 11am–6pm daily (last tour 5pm); Oct–Mar: 11am–5pm Mon–Sat (last tour 4:30pm) • Ajax Museum: Open Oct–Mar: 9:30am–5pm Mon–Sat; May–Sep: 9:30am–6pm Mon–Fri, 10am–5pm Sat–Sun • Admission charge*

Ajax Museum

Amsterdamse Bos

5 Ouderkerk aan de Amstel

There was no church in town until 1330 *(see p28)*, so people came instead to this picturesque riverside village to worship at the 11th-century Oude Kerk that stood here until it was destroyed by a storm in 1674. Convivial waterside cafés and restaurants are the chief lure these days, but you can also walk in the wooded garden of an 18th-century house, Wester Amstel, and visit an unexpected site: the Beth Haim Jewish cemetery. Amsterdam's Jews have been buried here since 1615, when they were forbidden burial in the city. ⊗ *Metro or train to Bijlmer, then bus 175, 300*

6 Het Amsterdamse Bos

Just a short bus, old-fashioned tram *(see p68)* or bike ride away, this attractive woodland park is a wonderful contrast to the city. Laid out on reclaimed land in the 1930s with the dual purpose of creating jobs for the unemployed and providing more recreation space, the park has woods and meadows, lakes and nature reserves. There is plenty to do: hire bicycles, go boating, eat pancakes, visit the bison and the goats and the Bos Museum, which describes the park and how it was built. ⊗ *Amstelveenseweg • Tram 24, Bus 170, 172, 174 • Open permanently*

7 Cobra Museum

This museum of modern art in residential Amstelveen is dedicated in part to the influential Dutch movement conceived in 1948. Its founders, including Dutchman Karel Appel *(see p47)* amalgamated the names of their home cities – Copenhagen, Brussels and Amsterdam – to create its name: CoBrA. They wanted to promote art that was spontaneous and inclusive, and were inspired by the work of primitives, children and the mentally ill. Paintings in the permanent collection are shown in changing thematic displays, augmented by temporary exhibitions. The light, spare building, by Wim Quist, opened in 1995. ⊗ *Sandbergplein 1–3, Amstelveen • Tram 5 to Binnenhof • 020 547 5050 • www.cobra-museum.nl • Open 11am– 5pm Tue–Sun • Closed 1 Jan, 30 Apr, 25 Dec • Admission charge*

8 Eastern Docklands

A mecca for architecture aficionados, this former docklands area to the east of Centraal Station has been transformed by ambitious urban regeneration plans. Spend a few hours admiring the bridge, inspired by a lizard, or the apartment block that resembles a whale. Also here is a row of houses, each designed by a different architect, and some inspired public art. Nearby are shops and cafés. ⊗ *Ferry from Centraal Station or Bus 42, 48; tram 10, 26*

City of Cyclists

Cycling comes as naturally to Amsterdammers as walking, and almost everyone has a bike. Theft is endemic, so snazzy, expensive models are avoided. Look out for: the huge bike shed at Centraal Station; bikes being dredged up from canals; obligatory tourists on yellow bikes; the eight-man "conference bike" and the heart-shaped "love bike".

Catch the Electrische Museumtramlijn at Haarlemmermeerstation (No.16 tram from Centraal Station).

9 NEMO

The most arresting feature of this interactive science and technology centre – the largest in the Netherlands – is the building itself. Designed by Renzo Piano, its harbour location (in the Eastern Islands) gave the impetus for a green copper structure resembling a ship. The views from the top deck will certainly appeal, even if the hands-on games, experiments and demonstrations, designed to entertain and educate both children and adults, do not. *Oosterdok 2 • Bus 22, 42, 43 • 020 531 3233 • www. e-nemo.nl • Open 10am–5pm Tue–Sun, also Mon during school holidays • Closed 1 Jan, 30 Apr, 25 Dec • Adm charge*

10 Frankendael

South of Plantage Middenlaan, Frankendael Park is Amsterdam's only remaining 17th-century country estate. The elegant Louis XIV–style Frankendael House, ornamental fountain by Ignatius van Logteren, historic formal gardens and coach buildings are all worth seeing. The main building hosts temporary exhibitions and there are two restaurants on the grounds, the Merkelbach (in the former coach house) and De Kas *(see p61)*. Guided tours of the house take place every Sunday at 11am. *Middenweg 72 • Tram 9 • 020 423 3930 • Garden open dawn–dusk*

NEMO

A Day Out with the Kids

Morning

Start by taking bus 22 or tram 7, 9, 10 or 14 to the **Tropenmuseum** *(see p123)*, a fascinating ethnographic museum which explores various non-Western cultures from around the world. Afterwards, enjoy an exotic lunch in the museum's café-restaurant, Ekeko, and don't forget to pop into the museum's shop to pick up a postcard or ethnic gift.

Afternoon

Outside the Tropenmuseum, pick up tram 7 or 10 to the Leidseplein and from there walk through the **Max Euweplein** *(see p116)* – pausing long enough to watch (or play) a giant game of chess – to the **Vondelpark** *(see p115)* where you can take in a music, dance or puppetry show at the open-air theatre. Nearby is the Kinderkookkafé where supervised children cook and serve up simple meals.

If park life is a big hit, head to the **Amsterdamse Bos** *(see p128)*. Be sure to stop at the visitor centre by the main entrance for a map of this sprawling woodland park. Rent bikes, canoe, horse-ride or take a ride on a historic tram. Don't miss the Fun Forest treetop course, or the working farm where children can feed the animals.

If there is time, take bus 170, 171 or 172 to Amstelveen and end the day with some modern art at the **Cobra Museum** *(see p128)*. Tram 5 or metro 51 will take you back to the city centre.

STREETSMART

AMSTERDAM'S TOP 10

Left **Euro notes** Right **Umbrellas on a rainy day**

🔟 Planning Your Trip

1 Choosing an Area
Most tourist hotels are to be found in one of three areas: the historic centre, the Museum Quarter and the atmospheric *Grachtengordel* (Canal Ring) with its gabled canal houses. Many business-oriented hotels are located a little further afield in the *Nieuw Zuid* (New South).

2 What to Pack
Be prepared for all weathers, and bring an umbrella, a waterproof jacket and a sweater – even in summer. Comfortable walking shoes are essential. Amsterdammers' dress style is casual and often creative. Few places insist on formality – casinos are an exception – but you can dress up for concerts and smart hotels and restaurants.

3 Passports and Other Documents
You must have a valid passport to enter the Netherlands. Citizens of EU countries, the USA, Australia and New Zealand need no visa as long as the stay is for less than three months. Passports must be valid for at least three months beyond the end of your stay. Citizens of other countries should consult their Dutch embassy or consulate for information. Everyone over 14 must carry valid means of identification at all times.

4 Customs
Apart from offensive weapons, plants and perishable foods, there are few limits on what EU nationals can import for personal use. Non-EU citizens can buy duty-free goods up to the current limit. Cats and dogs are allowed, provided they have a certificate of inoculation against rabies. Flower bulbs may be exported from the Netherlands; for the USA, a certificate of inspection from the Plant Protection Service is required. Bulbs are best mailed home; the dealer should carry out all the paperwork.

5 Currency
For security, bring a cash card or traveller's cheques. Make sure that your cash withdrawal card is accepted in the Netherlands – most are. Bring some euros to pay for immediate needs on arrival. There is no limit on how much currency you can bring in or take out of the country.

6 Driving
If you are planning to drive your own car, you must bring an EU or International Driver's Licence, valid insurance documents, proof of registration, road safety certificate and international identification disc. To hire a car, you must be 21 or over, with a valid driving licence and a credit card.

7 Electricity
The electricity supply in the Netherlands is 220 volts AC. British visitors should bring a two-pin adaptor for their three-pin plugs. Americans need to convert their equipment or buy a transformer, as Dutch wall sockets require a larger plug.

8 Time Difference
The Netherlands is on Central European Time, one hour ahead of GMT. Like the rest of the EU and the USA, it observes Daylight Saving Time, so it remains one hour ahead of the UK and six hours ahead of New York all year round.

9 Children's Needs
If you have very young children, it is best to carry them in baby slings; pushchairs are difficult to manoeuvre on the cobbled streets, and almost impossible to get on and off crowded trams and canal boats. Most places accept children, except for some expensive restaurants.

10 Public Holidays
Public holidays are as follows: New Year's Day (1 Jan); *Tweede Paasdag* (Easter Monday); *Koninginnedag* (30 Apr); *Bevrijdingsdag* (5 May); *Hemelvaartsdag* (Ascension Day); *Pinksteren* (Whitsun); *Eerste Kerstdag* (Christmas Day); *Tweede Kerstdag* (26 Dec).

Previous pages **Customers enjoying the view from waterfront tables outside Café de Jaren on Nieuwe Doelenstraat**

Left **Train at Centraal Station** Right **Arriving by road**

🔟 Arriving in Amsterdam

1 Schiphol Airport
Amsterdam's airport (official name Amsterdam Airport Schiphol) is efficient, modern and easy to use, with an incredible range of facilities from golf to gambling. There is a single terminal, with one level for Arrivals and another level for Departures. Signs are colour-coded: yellow for transfer desks and gates, green for amenities. *Flight information: 0900 0141 • www.schiphol.com*

2 From Schiphol by Train
The best and cheapest method of getting from the airport to the city is by rail – access is by escalator from the shopping plaza where the tickets are on sale. Trains run direct to Centraal Station every 4 to 7 minutes from 7am to midnight, then every hour. Journey time is 20 minutes.

3 From Schiphol by Bus
Instead of the train, you can take the smart Connexxion Airport-Hotel Shuttle (www.airporthotel shuttle.nl) from outside the main exit of the airport. It stops at over 100 hotels, leaving every 30 minutes between 6am and 9pm. You can also take a taxi, but it's hardly worth the expense, considering the ease of public transport.

4 Arriving by Train
You will arrive at Centraal Station. Its best feature is the 1e Klas café *(see p51)*; otherwise, it's crowded and prone to pickpockets, so head directly for the main entrance and Stations-plein. Here you will find the Amsterdam Tourist Board (VVV) and tram stops to the left and right, bus stops to the left. *Eurostar enquiries and reservations: 08705 186 186 • www.eurostar.com*

5 Arriving by Road
Drive on the right. Speed limits are 100 kph (60 mph) or 120 kph (75 mph) on motorways, 80 kph (50 mph) outside cities, and 50 kph (30 mph) in built-up areas. From the A10 ring road, the S-routes (marked by blue signs) take you to the centre of Amsterdam. *(See Driving p132.)*

6 Parking
The city centre is metered from 9am until at least 7pm (midnight in most places). Covered car parks (throughout the city, indicated by a white P on a blue background) are the best place to leave your car. Always empty it of valuables and leave the glove box open, as foreign-plated cars are regularly targeted. *Muziektheater Parking: Waterlooplein. • Map Q5 • Byzantium: Tesselschade-straat 1G. Map C5 • Euro-parking: Marnixstraat 250.*

Map J5 • www.q-park.nl • www.cition.nl

7 Arriving by Ferry
From London, the boat-train service, the Dutchflyer, offered by Stena Line via Harwich and the Hook of Holland departs twice daily and takes about 8 hours, and you will end your journey at Centraal Station. P&O ferries cross from Hull to Rotterdam or Zeebrugge and Dover to Calais, and DFDS Seaways has over-night crossings from Newcastle to IJmuiden. *DFDS: 08715 229955. www.dfds.co.uk • P&O: 08716 642121. www. poferries.com • Stena Line: 08445 762762. www. stenaline.co.uk*

8 Bus and Coach
From London's Victoria Coach Station, Eurolines coaches go via the Channel Tunnel or the ferry, taking between 9 and 12 hours to reach Amstel Station. *www.eurolines.co.uk*

9 Car Hire
As well as the major companies, try Diks or Kuperus *(see Driving p132).* *Diks: 020 662 3366. www.diks.net • Kuperus: 035 685 2000. www.autoverhuur-kuperus.nl*

10 Left Luggage
Schiphol has a staffed counter, open from 6am–10pm (0900 0141), and lockers. Centraal Station has 24-hour lockers.

Left **Amsterdam Tourist Board** Right **Reference books in an Amsterdam library**

Sources of Information

1 Amsterdam Tourist Board

Still universally known by its old name, VVV, the Tourist Board has three offices in the city *(see below)*. At these you will find free maps, and leaflets on just about everything – including walks, canal tours, sights, exhibitions, transport and accommodation. Multi-lingual staff will give advice, change money, arrange excursions and – for a fee – book tickets and hotels. Here you can also buy the popular I amsterdam Card and *Museumkaart (see p136)*.
🕾 *020 201 8800*
• *www.iamsterdam.com*

2 Tourist Offices

There are three VVV offices in Amsterdam itself: at Centraal Station (Platform 28), at Stationsplein 10 (in front of the station), and at Stadhouderskade (next to the Canalbus ticket booth). There are also offices at Schiphol Airport (Holland Tourist Information Arrivals 2). Other key tourist offices are located on Museumplein, Paulus Potterstraat 8 and inside Gays and Gadgets, the gay novelty store at Spuistrat 44.

3 Websites

The Amsterdam Tourist Board's official website is www. iamsterdam.com. The City of Amsterdam has its own Dutch-language website, www.amsterdam.nl. All of these have useful, up-to-date information on accommodation, events, exhibitions, shopping and travel (you can also book hotel rooms online). To find out what's on, visit www.aub.nl/amsterdam. The majority of the city's museums and attractions have their own websites.

4 NBTC (Netherlands Board of Tourism and Conventions)

You can pick up the NBTC's own maps, information leaflets and brochures at any of its offices throughout the world. Visit your nearest branch before you travel.
🕾 *www.holland.com*

5 Amsterdam Hotel Service

The friendly staff at this independent organization will make hotel reservations (even last-minute ones), book excursions and proffer helpful advice. 🕾 *Damrak 7* • *Map P1* • *020 520 7000* • *www.amsterdamhotelservice.com*

6 Accommodation

To book hotels before you travel (which is advisable), contact the Amsterdam Reservation Center, a branch of the Amsterdam Tourist Board. 🕾 *PO Box 3901, NL–1001 AS Amsterdam* • *020 551 2525* • *reservations@atcb.nl or www.iamsterdam.com*

7 Publications

The best listings magazine in Dutch is *Uitkrant*. Published monthly, it is free and widely available. The Tourist Board publishes *Day by Day*, a monthly listings magazine in English (on sale in news-agents and free in hotels and restaurants).

8 AUB Ticketshop

For information on plays and concerts, or to make reservations (for a small fee), contact Amsterdam Uitburo. Between noon–7:30pm, tickets are sold for same-day shows at reduced prices. 🕾 *Leidseplein 26* • *www.amsterdamsuitburo. nl* • *Map C5* • *0900 0191*

9 Newspapers

You will find the best selection of foreign daily and Sunday newspapers at Athenaeum Nieuws-centrum, Waterstone's and the American Book Center. 🕾 *Athenaeum Nieuwscentrum: Spui 14–16. Map M5* • *Waterstone's: Kalverstraat 152. Map M5* • *American Book Center: Spui 12. Map M5*

10 Libraries

Only residents can borrow books, but a visit to the OBA (Amsterdam Public Library) is still worthwhile for the free Wi-Fi and foreign-language books and newspapers. 🕾 *Oosterdokskade 143* • *Map R2* • *020 523 0900* • *Open 10am–10pm daily*

For alternative listings, check out the excellent www.underwateramsterdam.com

Left **Bicycles secured in a bike rack** Right **Trams**

Getting Around

1 Trams
Trams run from 6am (6:30am Sat–Sun) till midnight. Most start at Centraal Station. For routes, see the map on the back cover of this book. You can buy tickets in advance from the GVB *(see below)*, or on board the tram itself.

2 Buses
Most buses start at Centraal Station. A few follow similar routes, but buses also go to areas not covered by trams; again, see the map at the back. Buses have the same ticketing system as trams. The City Centre line bus runs every 30 minutes daily, down Prinsengracht, up the Amstel, past Waterlooplein and Nieuwemarkt. A limited night service runs from midnight to 5:30am.

3 Metro
Serving more remote parts of the city, the Metro has only four lines, all terminating at Centraal Station. There are four other stations in the central area: Amsterdam CS, Nieuwmarkt, Waterlooplein and Weesperplein. It is best to avoid taking the Metro late at night, especially if you are travelling alone.

4 Tickets
The *OV Chipkaart* (Public Transport Smartcard) is a card that allows you to travel with any means of public transport throughout the Netherlands. Three cards are available – Personal (reloadable with credit or a season ticket), Anonymous (reloadable with credit only) and Disposable (fixed credit). When boarding, hold the card up to the card reader (either built into the gate or on a free-standing yellow pillar). At the end of the journey, hold the card up to the reader again. ✆ *GVB: Stationsplein 14 • Map P1 • 0900 9292 • www.gvb.nl • www.ov-chipkaart.nl*

5 Taxis
You can try to hail taxis in the street, but finding one in the centre is usually easy, as there are plenty of taxi ranks: at Centraal Station, Dam Square, Elandsgracht, Leidseplein, Muziektheater, Nieuwmarkt and Rembrandtplein. There is also a 24-hour phone service, Taxicentrale. ✆ *Taxicentrale: 020 777 7777 or 020 650 6506*

6 Driving
The city centre has a complex one-way system, its roads are dominated by trams and cyclists, and parking is limited – and expensive, all good reasons to avoid driving. If you have to, park in a car park or on a meter *(see p133)*.

7 Bicycle Hire
You will never be very far from a bicycle hire shop in this city of cyclists: Bike City, Holland Rent-a-Bike and Take-a-Bike are all conveniently central. Bike theft is rife, so secure your bike carefully when you park it. ✆ *Bike City: Bloemgracht 70. Map K2. 020 626 3721 • Holland Rent-a-Bike. Damrak 247. Map N2. 020 622 3207 • Macbike: Stationsplein 5. Map P1. 020 620 0985*

8 Canal Bikes
These two- or four-person pedaloes provide a fun way of getting around. There are four moorings in central Amsterdam, where you can collect or leave the bikes all year round. ✆ *020 623 9886 • www.canal.nl*

9 Trains
Nederlandse Spoorwegen, the Dutch national rail company, is renowned for its clean, punctual trains and reasonable fares. Contact the OVR (Openbaar Vervoer Reisinformatie) for information. ✆ *OVR: 0900 9292 • www.9292ov.nl*

10 Walking
Amsterdam is a great city for walking *(see pp64–5)*. The main pedestrian hazards are bicycles, trams and cobbled streets, so keep clear of cycle lanes, take care crossing tram tracks, and wear comfortable, flat shoes.

Left **Canal tour** Right **Yellow bicycle riders**

ᵀᴼᴾ10 Sightseeing

1 I amsterdam Card
Available from hotels and Amsterdam Tourist Board offices, the I amsterdam Card represents good value for money, at €40, €50 and €60 for one, two and three days respectively. It entitles the holder to free public transport, free admission to many museums, a free canal tour, and discounts at a variety of restaurants and other attractions.
🌐 www.iamsterdam.com

2 Museumkaart
Most museums are covered by the I amsterdam Card *(see above)*. If you want to visit more, you need the *Museumkaart* (Museum Card), which buys a year's admission to over 400 museums throughout the Netherlands. You will recoup the cost (€40). Available from all Amsterdam Tourist Board offices and participating museums.

3 Cultureel Jongeren Paspoort (CJP)
The CJP gives under-30-year-olds discounted admission to theatres, museums and other attractions. It is available from the offices of the Amsterdam Tourist Board, the AUB Uitburo ticket shop *(see p134)*, and Stayokay hostels.

4 Canal Tours
Cruises can either be booked direct with the operator or through the Amsterdam Tourist Board. Many start from Centraal Station. For something different, board the Floating Dutchman amphibious bus. 🛈 *Lovers: Prins Hendrikkade 25. Map P1. 020 530 5412. www.lovers. nl • Amsterdam Canal Cruises: Map D6. 020 679 1370. www.amsterdam canalcruises.nl • Kooij: Rokin 125 (opposite). Map N5. 020 623 3810. www. rederijkooij.nl • Floating Dutchman: 020 316 3951. www.floatingdutchman.nl*

5 Hop on Hop off Museum Line
The Hop on Hop off Museum Line offers two routes to different museums. The day ticket also entitles you to discounted museum admission. 🛈 *Stationsplein 8 • Map P1 • 020 530 1090 • www.lovers.nl*

6 Canalbus
Another frequent hop-on, hop-off canal boat, with discounts included in the ticket price. Choose one of three routes, with a total of 17 stops. A one-day ticket entitles you to hop on and off as many times as you like. 🛈 *Weteringschans 24 • Map D5 • 020 623 9886 • www.canal.nl*

7 Water Taxi
More private cruisers than taxis. The cost is around €110 an hour for an 8-seater. 🛈 *Stationsplein 8 • Map P1 • 020 535 6363 • www.water-taxi.nl*

8 Koetstaxi
Sightseeing by horse-drawn carriage. Tours start at Dam Square and last 20–60 minutes, or use their taxi service and order a taxi to take you to town. 🛈 *020 691 3478 • www.koetstaxi.nl*

9 Bicycle Tours
Yellow Bike offers two guided bicycle tours for up to 12 people: a 2-hour city tour and 4-hour countryside tour. You can book direct through Yellow Bike, or through the Amsterdam Tourist Board. 🛈 *Yellow Bike: 020 620 6940 • www.yellowbike.nl*

10 Walking Tours
The Amsterdam Tourist Board offers a range of walking tours. Urban Home & Garden Tours visit private and public canal houses *(see p105)*. Mee in Mokum give fresh insights into historic Amsterdam. Architectour/ Archivisie examine the historical and modern architecture. Amsterdam City Walks focus more on history. 🛈 *Urban Home & Garden Tours: 020 688 1243. www.uhgt.nl • Mee in Mokum: 020 625 1390. www.gildeamsterdam.nl • Architectour/Archivisie: 020 625 9123 • Amsterdam City Walks: 061 825 7014. www.amsterdamcitywalks. com*

Left **Street stall selling herring** Right **Street performer**

10 Amsterdam on a Budget

1 Hostels and Camping

There are several popular youth hostels *(see box)*. Vondelpark is especially recommended, with private rooms as well as dormitories. Vliegenbos is a designated youth campsite. The Amsterdamse Bos campsite also has wooden cabins for hire, and, like Gaasper, is suited to families. *(See also Budget Hotels, p149).*

2 Discount Cards

Under-26-year-olds can apply for a CJP for bargains on some performing arts tickets *(see p136)*. The I amsterdam Card represents good value for money. The *Museumkaart* allows free admission to more than 400 museums in the Netherlands *(see p136)*.

3 OBA

The main branch of the Amsterdam public library (OBA) is a great place to hang out on a rainy afternoon. Read a magazine, check your email free of charge or just take in the view of the city *(see p134)*.

4 Markets

The outdoor markets of Albert Cuypmarkt, Waterlooplein and Noordermarkt, and the indoor bargain basement Rommelmarkt, are all places where you can find food, clothing and bric-a-brac for next to nothing *(see pp62–3)*.

5 Free Sights

Special places that can be visited free of charge include: the Civic Guards Gallery of the Amsterdam Museum *(see p26)*; *hofjes (see p92)*; the Begijnhof *(see p22)*; Fo Guang Shan Temple *(see p81)*; the Rijksmuseum Garden *(see p14)*; and Bloemenmarkt *(see p109)*.

6 Free Music

There is plenty of music in the air, from the carillons of the Westertoren, Zuidertoren and Munttoren, to barrel organs, street performers and live bands in late-night bars. Free lunchtime concerts are held from September to early June at the Concertgebouw (Wed), Stopera (Tue in winter) and Thomaskerk (alternate Tuesdays).

7 Free Film

There are free performances at the Vondelpark's open-air theatre from June to August *(see p71)*.

8 Tickets

To see what's on, consult *Uitkrant* and *Day by Day*. The best place to book tickets is AUB in Leidseplein *(see p134)*.

9 Parks

Amsterdam's parks offer endless free entertainment, from theatre and concerts in the Vondelpark to the miniature train in Amstelpark, or just feeding the goats in Amsterdamse Bos.

10 Cheap Eats

You can keep hunger at bay without entering a restaurant in Amsterdam, with its many food stalls selling raw herring, smoked fish, chips with mayonnaise, *belegde broodjes* (filled bread rolls), waffles, pancakes and delicious, sugary *poffertjes* – and there are plenty of cheap cafés.

Hostels and Campsites

Hans Brinker
Kerkstraat 136 • 020 622 0687 • www.hans-brinker.com

The Bulldog
Oudezijds Voorburgwal 218–220 • 020 620 3822 • www.bulldoghotel.com

Flying Pig Palace
Vossiusstraat 46 • 020 400 4187 • www.flyingpig.nl

Stayokay Vondelpark
Zandpad 5 • 020 589 8996 • www.stayokay.com

Amsterdamse Bos Camping
Kleine Noorddijk 1, Amstelveen • 020 641 6868 • www.camping amsterdamsebos.nl

Gaasper Camping
Loosdrechtdreef 7 • 020 696 7326 • www.gaaspercamping.nl

Vliegenbos Camping
Meeuwenlaan 138 • 020 636 8855 • www.vliegenbos.com

Left **Cheese on a stall in the Albert Cuypmarkt** Right **Tulips at Amsterdam's Bloemenmarkt**

TOP 10 Shopping Tips

1 Areas
Each shopping area has its own special character. De Negen Straatjes, the Jordaan and Haarlemmerbuurt have bric-a-brac and speciality shops. The Spiegelkwartier and Rokin are the places for art and antiques. Most chain stores are in Kalverstraat and Nieuwendijk. Leidsestraat and Utrechtsestraat have more upmarket boutiques, and PC Hooftstraat is the home of designer fashion.

2 Hours
By city law, shop-keepers can trade from 7am–10pm daily. Generally, shops open from 10am–6pm Tue, Wed and Fri, from 10am–9pm on Thu, from 10am–5pm on Sat, and from 1–6pm on Mon (although most department stores open at 11am). Many shops also open from noon to 6pm on Sun.

3 Tax-free Shopping
Most marked prices include 19 per cent VAT. Global Refund entitles non-EU residents to a percentage back over a minimum figure of €50 (more you spend, the higher the percentage), bought at one shop on the same day and exported within 90 days. If the shop has 'Tax-free' status, collect a Global Refund Cheque, have it stamped by Customs on your departure, and claim your refund when you leave the EU.

4 Sales
January and July are the traditional months for end-of-season sales, when you are likely to find some great bargains. Some shops have an almost permanent sale rail. *Korting* means reductions are being offered. The Dutch for sale is *uitverkoop*.

5 What to Buy
Amsterdam shopping is very cosmopolitan. It spans designer fashion and off-beat second-hand clothes, valuable antiques and colourful Indonesian beads. For a flavour of the city, you might be tempted by Dutch chocolate, cheese, *haring* (raw herring), beer or *jenever* or, for something less ephemeral, Delftware or diamonds.

6 Department Stores and Malls
Compared to its speciality shops, Amsterdam's department stores seem run-of-the-mill. On the corner of Dam Square and Damrak, De Bijenkorf is the most famous. More exclusive, however, are Maison de Bonneterie and Metz & Co. The city's first mall, Magna Plaza, has several floors of boutiques and cafés in a converted post office.

7 Speciality Shops
It is these quirky little shops devoted to specific items – from candles to toothbrushes – that make shopping in Amsterdam such a joy. Although they crop up throughout the city, they are thickest on the ground in De Negen Straatjes (*see p104*).

8 Art and Antiques
The Spiegelkwartier is the heart of the art and antiques trade. Here, a host of dealers specialize in a variety of objects from Delftware and glass to icons and tribal art (*see p112*).

9 Diamonds
The companies listed below guarantee quality and will give you expert advice on the cut, carat, colour and size of your diamond. ✆ *Gassan Dam Square: Rokin 1. Map N3. 020 624 5787 • Coster Diamonds: Paulus Potterstraat 2–6. Map C5. 020 305 5555 • Gassan Diamonds: Nieuwe Uilenburgerstraat 173–5. Map Q4. 020 622 5333*

10 Bulbs and Flowers
The Dutch love flowers. For the best selection of cut flowers and bulbs, visit Amsterdam's famous floating market, Bloemenmarkt (*see p108*). Depending on the harshness of the winter, bulbs are usually available between June and late December, but it is a good idea to check your own country's import regulations before exporting (*see p132*).

⯈ *For shops, markets and souvenirs* See pp62–3

Left **Boonstra taxi service** Right **Disabled access sign**

Amsterdam for the Disabled

1 Organizations
Amsterdam's narrow, cobbled streets, uneven pavements, and old buildings with small entrances and steep stairs, make it a difficult city for disabled people to get around. For general information and advice, contact TTFA (Travel & Tourism for All) or SGOA (Stichting Gehandicapten Overleg Amsterdam). *TTFA: www.toegankelijkamster dam.nl • SGOA: Plantage Middenlaan 14I, 1018 DD. Map F4. 020 752 5140.*

2 Leaflets
Useful leaflets on hotels, restaurants, museums and attractions, guided tours and excursions for people with disabilities are available from the Amsterdam Tourist Office and the AUB (Amsterdam Uitburo) *(see p134)*. You can also pick up an excellent booklet called Rail Travel for the Disabled from Centraal Station.

3 Accommodation
For such a progressive city, Amsterdam's hotels are remarkably cavalier about the needs of disabled people; very few have special facilities. Some modern hotels have adapted rooms, but old buildings and converted canal houses often have steep staircases and no lift. The accommodation booklet of the Amsterdam Tourist Office lists hotels with disabled facilities,

but be sure that they meet your needs before you make a reservation.

4 Public Transport
Most trams are accessible for wheelchair users, with central doors at pavement level. The metro is wheelchair-friendly, with lifts at every station. For the visually impaired, there is a PA system that announces every stop. The NS (Dutch Railway) offers assistance when travelling by train (call 030 235 7823). Avoid public transport at rush hour.

5 Taxis
A folded wheelchair will fit into most taxis, but Amsterdam has a private service, Boonstra, specially designed for wheelchair users. It costs the same as a regular cab, but you need to book at least 48 hours in advance. *Prins Bernhardkade 1, Halfweg • 020 613 4134 • 9am–6pm Mon to Sat*

6 Museums
Most museums have adequate facilities for disabled people, including wide entrances, ramps, lifts and adapted toilets, although canalhouse museums like the Ons' Lieve Heer op Solder, Van Loon and Willet-Holthuysen have no upper-floor wheelchair access. Staff are usually very helpful, but it's always a good idea to telephone before you visit.

7 Restaurants
It's possible to get a wheelchair into most ground-floor restaurants, but only a handful have disabled toilet facilities. Again, it's wise to phone ahead to check that a wheelchair user can be accommodated.

8 Wheelchair Hire
If you need to rent a wheelchair in Amsterdam, go to the Toegankelijk Amsterdam (Accessible Amsterdam) website, click on "Assistance and Facilities" and then "Wheelchair rental" for a list of hire places. Be sure to book well in advance, particularly in the holiday season. *Toegankelijk Amsterdam: www.toegankelijkamster dam.nl*

9 Guided Tours
Tours and Travel Services offer bus tours around Amsterdam and day-trips throughout the Netherlands using buses suitable for wheelchairs. *Tours & Travel Services: TT Melissaweg 15, 1033 SP Amsterdam. 020 635 3110. www.tandts.nl*

10 Impaired Sight
Audio tours of museums and other tourist attractions are increasingly available. The Dedicon has magazines etc. for the partially sighted. *0486 486 486 • Dedicon: www.dedicon.nl • public transport: 0900 9292*

Left **Pedestrian-free cycle lane** Right **Queue at Rijksmuseum**

🔟 Things to Avoid

1 Street Crime
Beware pickpockets in crowded places like Centraal Station, the Red Light District, Damrak and Leidseplein. Never keep money in your back pocket, or leave your handbag exposed. At night, avoid the junkie-riddled fringes of the Red Light District, especially around Zeedijk, as well as the area around Nieuwendijk between Damrak and Spuistraat.

2 Bicycle Theft
Bicycle theft is rife in Amsterdam. Some are stolen for profit, others on the principle that "someone stole mine, so I'll steal someone else's". Always secure both front wheel and frame to an immovable object with a U-shaped lock.

3 Medical Problems
EU nationals are entitled to receive dental and medical treatment in the Netherlands at a reduced charge. To cover this, British visitors should bring a European Health Insurance Card (EHIC), available from post offices. It is also sensible to take out private travel insurance before you leave, to cover medical emergencies and repatriation *(see p142)*.

4 Dog Mess
It's a strange paradox that the famously house-proud Dutch should put up with fouled streets in their capital city (other towns and cities are much cleaner). A few years ago the problem was dire; it's much better now, but you still need to look where you walk.

5 Losing Possessions
For lost property at Schiphol Airport, call 020 794 0800. For items left on a train, call 0900 321 2100, 8am–8pm Mon–Fri. For trams, buses or the Metro, call 0900 8011, 9am–4pm Mon–Fri.

6 Infringing Drug Laws
Amsterdam's enlightened attitude to soft drugs should not be misconstrued. "Coffeeshops" are the only places where buying and using small quantities of soft drugs is tolerated. Elsewhere – in the street, or in other bars, clubs, cafés and restaurants – smoking is frowned on.

7 Causing Offence
As the expression "going Dutch" indicates, Amsterdammers will usually share the bill in a restaurant. If you dine at someone's home, bring a small gift such as flowers or chocolates for the host. Try not to annoy cyclists by walking in cycle lanes. Though most Amsterdammers speak excellent English, a few words in Dutch will go down well *(see pp158–9)*. Don't cause offence by taking photographs of the prostitutes in their windows.

8 Mosquitoes
Summertime heralds the arrival of these irritating insects, attracted to the canal waters. Arm yourself with repellent and a good bite cream.

9 Getting Caught Short
Though there are (albeit very public) men's conveniences on some streets, women are very poorly provided for. Instead, it is acceptable practice to head for the nearest bar or café. You might buy a drink in return, but usually you are not obliged to. Public toilets in stations and museums are staffed by attendants who insist on a tip in a saucer.

10 Tourist Hordes
Amsterdam is busy all year round, but especially from April to September, when you should book up your accommodation well before you plan to visit. Canal cruises and other tours should be booked on arrival. Places like the Rijksmuseum and Anne Frank House attract long queues. Order tickets on-line or arrive early in the day, or late, if visiting the Anne Frank House. Other popular tourist sights see more visitors arriving in the early morning.

 Smoking is now banned in all public spaces, hotels, restaurants and cafés.

Left **OBA (Amsterdam Public Library)** Right **Post boxes**

Banking and Communications

Currency
In 2002, the Dutch guilder became obsolete and the euro became the official currency of the Netherlands. Euro banknotes have seven denominations: 5, 10, 20, 50, 100, 200 and 500. There are also eight coin denominations: 1 and 2 euros, and 1, 2, 5, 10, 20 and 50 cents. Most shops have now stopped using 1- and 2-cent coins and purchases are rounded up or down. Check exchange rates before you travel.

Credit Cards
Major cards including Amex are widely accepted throughout Amsterdam, and you should have no difficulty paying for most things with credit cards – it's always wise to check. Some restaurants do not accept credit cards, and it is common practice to pay small amounts in cash, so keep some on you.

Cash Dispensers
Amsterdam has no shortage of cash dispensers, many of which will function in several languages.

Travellers' Cheques
Travellers' cheques are a safe way of carrying money abroad, and can be exchanged for cash in banks and used to pay hotel bills, as well as being widely accepted in retail outlets. Choose a well-known company such as American Express or Thomas Cook.

Changing Money
You can change money in banks, bureaux de change, post offices and American Express offices. To avoid high commission charges, stay clear of independent bureaux de change (like those on Leidsestraat) and choose the official GWK bureaux de change or the post office Postbank. Avoid changing money in hotels.

Postal Services
The national postal service is PostNL, with locations recognizable by their orange logo. The main post office is on Singel, and another central point is Waterlooplein 10. Most post offices are located within shops. Stamps can also be bought at Albert Heijn, tobacco shops and souvenir shops. ✆ *Singel 250 • Map M3 • 0900 767 8526 • Open 7:30am–6:30pm Mon–Fri, 7:30am–5pm Sat*

Internet Cafés
You can pick up and send emails, or just surf, for free at the OBA (Amsterdam Public Library), *(see p134)*. There are several other Internet cafés in town, and some hotels and bars also have terminals.

✆ *Freeworld: Nieuwendijk 30. • Map N1 • 020 620 0902 • Open 9am–1am daily*

Telephones
Most public telephones (which are green, with the KPN Telecom logo) require a phonecard – which you can buy at post offices, supermarkets, newsagents and stations – or credit card. The international dialling code for The Netherlands is 00 31. The code for Amsterdam is 020 – you can drop this if you are dialling a local number.

Television
Ask a Dutch child where he or she learned to speak such good, idiomatic English, and the answer is likely to be "from the television". British and American imports on Dutch channels are subtitled rather than dubbed, and cable TV brings about 35 stations from around Europe, plus America's CNN. Most of the city's hotels are equipped with cable TV.

Radio
For classical music, tune in to Dutch Radio 4 (92.4 MHz); for pop music to 3FM (91.5 MHz). There are also several independent music stations, mostly aimed at the young. News is broadcast on Radio 1 (88.5 MHz).

Left **Prescriptions at an *apotheek*** Right **A&E dept, Onze Lieve Vrouwe Gasthuis**

Security and Health

1 Emergency
Dial 112 if you need police, ambulance or fire brigade. English-speaking operators man the 24-hour switchboard, and you can phone free from a call box.

2 Personal Safety
Don't carry your passport, ticket and other valuables around with you. At night, stick to well-lit streets, avoiding dodgy areas like De Pijp, Nieuwendijk and the seediest part of the Red Light District around Zeedijk. Everyone over 14 years must carry a valid means of identification at all times.

3 Theft
Insure your possessions. Should you have anything stolen, report it immediately to the police and ask for a copy of the police report for your insurers. If your passport is stolen, you must also contact your consulate or embassy as soon as possible.

4 Police
The main police stations are located in Prinsengracht, Beurssraat, Lijnbaansgracht and Nieuwezijds Voorburgwal.
Prinsengracht 1109. Map E5 • Beursstraat 33. Map P2 • Lijnbaansgracht 219. Map C5 • Nieuwezijds Voorburgwal 104. Map M4 • Central No.: 0900 8844; Emergency: 112

5 Victim Support
Get help from the Amsterdam Tourist Assistance Service (ATAS). Advies-en Steunpunt helps victims of rape and sexual assault. *Amsterdam Tourist Assistance Service: Nieuwezijds Voorburgwal 104–8. 020 625 3246 • Advies-en Steunpunt. 020 611 6022*

6 Hospitals
Emergency (EHBO-post) departments can be found at any hospital (ziekenhuis). *AMC (Academisch Medisch Centrum Universiteit van Amsterdam): Meibergdreef 9. 020 566 9111 • Boven het IJ Hospital: Statenjachtstraat 1. 020 634 6346 OLVG (Onze Lieve Vrouwe Gasthuis): Oosterpark 9. 020 566 9111 • Emergencies: Gravesandeplein 16. Map G6 • 020 599 9111 • VU Medical Centre: De Boelelaan 1117; 020 444 4444 • Sint Lucas Andreas Hospital: Jan Tooropstraat 164; 020 510 8911*

7 Pharmacies
For non-prescription drugs or toiletries, go to a chemist (drogist). To have a prescription made up, go to a pharmacy (apotheek). Normal opening times are 8:30am–5:30pm Mon–Fri.

8 Doctors and Dentists
Your hotel, local pharmacy or tourist office will direct you to an English-speaking doctor or dentist, as will the GP Service Post Foundation Amsterdam (SHDA). EU citizens are entitled to reductions on medical and dental treatment *(see p140)*. *SHDA: 088 003 0600. www.shda.nl*

9 Embassies and Consulates
Most embassies are in The Hague, but some countries have consular facilities in Amsterdam. *UK Consulate: Koningslaan 44. 020 676 4343. www.britain.nl • US Consulate: Museumplein 19. 020 575 5309. www. amsterdam.usconsulate.gov*

10 Sexual Health
The Dutch take sexual health seriously: prostitutes are subjected to rigorous checks. Should you contract a sexually transmitted disease, the GGD provides a Mon–Fri walk-in clinic; phone for details. An HIV checkpoint, by appointment only, is run by the Servicepunt HIV Vereniging on Friday evenings. They also operate an HIV helpline from 2–10pm Thu–Tue. The Schorer Stichting provides information for gays. *GGD: Weesperplein 1. Map F5. 020 555 5822 • Servicepunt HIV Vereniging: Eerste Helmersstraat 17. Map C5. Helpline: 020 689 2577 • SAD Schorer Stichting: 020 573 9444 • AIDS-STD Helpline: 0900 204 2040*

Left **Inside the UvA Main Library** Right **VU Boekhandel**

TOP 10 Amsterdam for Students

1 UvA Courses
The largest university with buildings in the centre, UvA (Universiteit van Amsterdam) offers English-language International Study Programs in a range of subjects from undergraduate level upwards. For information, contact the Office of Foreign Relations. ✪ *Office of Foreign Relations: Binnengasthuisstraat 9. • Map N5 • 020 525 8080 • www.uva.nl*

2 VU Courses
In a suburb of Amsterdam, VU (Vrije Universiteit) runs English-language courses in economics, law, arts and social sciences for exchange or contract students (whose home university has no official exchange relationship with the VU). ✪ *VU: De Boelelaan 1105, Room OE-49. 020 598 9898 • www.vu.nl*

3 Accommodation
ASVA (UvA's student union) helps students find lodgings. If you are studying at VU, the university has a guest-house in Uilenstede. Alternatively, SRVU, the VU students' union, will help you. ✪ *ASVA: Binnengasthuisstraat 9. Map N5. 020 525 2926 • SRVU: De Boelelaan 1083A. 020 598 9422 • www.srvu.org*

4 Student Cards
Producing your student union or ISIC rail-card in Amsterdam does not guarantee discounted prices, and only Dutch students are entitled to the *OV Jaarkaart*, which gives them free use of public transport. Anyone under the age of 26 is eligible for a *Cultureel Jongeren Paspoort (see p136)*, which costs €12.50 from Tourist Offices or the AUB *(see p134)*.

5 Unions
Foreign students will find ASVA the most useful of the various Dutch student unions. It offers all kinds of assistance, including an accommodation service. SRVU will also give VU students help and advice *(see above)*. ✪ *ASVA: Binnengasthuisstraat 9 • Map N5 • 020 525 2926*

6 Services for Foreign Students
An independent organization, the FSS (Foreign Student Service) provides advice, support and help for foreign students, as well as arranging social events. Under the auspices of the UvA, the International Student Network (ISN) is a group of students that provides mentors to introduce foreigners and freshmen to university life. ✪ *FSS: Oranje Nassaulaan 5. 020 671 5915. Map A6 • ISN: 020 525 3721. info@isn-amsterdam.nl. www.isn-amsterdam.nl • www.foreignstudents.nl*

7 Summer Courses
The UvA and VU both offer academic courses over the summer months. The Felix Meritis Foundation also holds its own Amsterdam-Maastricht Summer University, with courses in arts and sciences. ✪ *www.uva.nl • www.vu.nl • www.amsu.edu*

8 Bookshops
Most major bookshops stock English textbooks, but the best academic bookshop is VU Boekhandel. ✪ *VU Boekhandel: De Boelelaan 1105 • 020 598 4000*

9 Libraries
To borrow from the UvA Main Library, you need a *Universiteit Bibliotheek* card. Foreign students are eligible if they are studying in the city for at least three months. To borrow from the VU Main Library, you must become a member. ✪ *UvA Main Library: Singel 425. Map M5. 020 525 2301 • VU Main Library: De Boelelaan 1105. 020 598 5200*

10 Visas
All foreign students who plan to stay in the country for longer than three months must register with the *Vreemdelingenpolitie* (Foreign Police) within three days of arrival. They must then apply for a MVV (residence permit) and register with the civil registry. ✪ *www.ind.nl*

Left **Crown Plaza Amsterdam American** Right **NH Grand Hotel Krasnapolsky**

TOP 10 Luxury Hotels

1 Amstel Inter-Continental
Rub shoulders with monarchs and movie stars in Amsterdam's grandest hotel, which just oozes opulence, from the spectacular hall to the pampering bedrooms. Enjoy the state-of-the-art gym, private motor launch and one-Michelin-starred restaurant – just don't think about the bill. ✆ *Professor Tulpplein 1, 1018 GX • Map F5 • 020 622 6060 • www.intercontinental.com • Dis. access • €€€€€*

2 The Dylan
Tucked behind the historical façades of Keizersgracht's canal houses, the Dylan Hotel exudes elegance. Contemporary meets classic design, with a manicured courtyard at its heart and a restaurant, Vinkeles, that boasts a Michelin Star *(see p103)*. ✆ *Keizersgracht 384, 1016 GB • Map L4 • 020 530 2010 • www.dylan amsterdam.com • €€€€€*

3 Grand Amsterdam (Sofitel Legend)
A sense of history pervades this hotel on the fringes of the Red Light District: the 17th-century building was designed for the Admiralty. It offers five-star comfort and is home to Bridges Restaurant *(see p60)*. ✆ *Oudezijds Voorburgwal 197, 1012 EX • Map N4 • 020 555 3111 • www.thegrand.nl • Dis. access • €€€€€*

4 Pulitzer
Combining 21st-century chic with beams and bare bricks, the Pulitzer is an innovative conversion of 25 canal houses, celebrated for its art exhibitions, courtyard garden and outstanding wine cellar. ✆ *Prinsengracht 315–31, 1016 GZ • Map K3 • 020 523 5235 • www.hotelpulitzer amsterdam.nl • €€€€€*

5 NH Grand Hotel Krasnapolsky
This monumental hotel, with 468 rooms and 36 apartments, has come a long way from its beginnings as a humble coffee-shop *(see p35)*. The facilities are phenomenal. The original cast-iron and glass Winter Garden breakfast room is stunning. ✆ *Dam 9, 1012 JS • Map N3 • 020 554 9111 • www.nh-hotels.com • Dis.access • €€€€€*

6 De l'Europe
Originally built in 1896, De l'Europe surrounds visitors with original works of the Dutch Masters from the private collection of Alfred "Freddy" Heineken. Spacious rooms with empire furnishings are the epitome of plush. ✆ *Nieuwe Doelenstraat 2–14, 1012 CP • Map N5 • 020 531 1777 • www.leurope.nl • Dis.access • €€€€€*

7 NH Barbizon Palace
Behind a dull façade, a row of 17th-century houses – 19 in all – have been knocked together to create a luxurious hotel. ✆ *Prins Hendrikkade 59–72, 1012 AD • Map P1 • 020 556 4564 • www.nh-hotels. com • Dis.access • €€€€€*

8 Amsterdam American
This landmark hotel in a splendid Art Nouveau building is for those who want to be close to the action. *(see p101).* ✆ *Leidsekade 97, 1017 PN • Map C5 • 020 556 3000 • www.edenamsterdam americanhotel.com • €€€€*

9 The College Hotel
This luxurious "training hotel" for students in the hospitality industry occupies an old school building dating from 1895. Rooms and suites are elegant and include custom-made furniture and Wi-Fi. There is a restaurant, bar and garden. ✆ *Roelof Hartstraat 1, 1071 VE • Map C6 • 020 571 1511 • www. thecollegehotel.com • €€€€€*

10 Banks Mansion
This exquisite hotel, formerly a bank, successfully fulfills its concept of being a "home from home". Most notably, many of the facilities – Internet access, the rooms' private bar, morning paper and appetisers from the hotel lounge – are included in the price. ✆ *Herengracht 519–25, 1017 BV • Map N5 • 020 420 0055 • www. carlton.nl/banksmansion • €€€€€*

Note: *Unless otherwise stated, all hotels accept credit cards and have en-suite bathrooms.*

Price Categories

For a standard, double room per night (with breakfast if included), taxes and extra charges.

€	under €90
€€	€90–140
€€€	€140–200
€€€€	€200–250
€€€€€	over €250

Lloyd Hotel

TOP 10 Hotels with Character

1 Fusion Suites 40
One of the more unusual hotels in Amsterdam, each suite is decorated in its own distinctive style, from the Indian suite to the Modern Classic. The location is ideal – close to Museumplein, smart shopping streets, Vondelpark and bustling Leidseplein. ✆ *Roemer Visscherstraat 40, 1054 EZ • Map C5 • 020 618 4642 • www.fusionsuites.com • €€€€€*

2 Ambassade
Overlooking the Herengracht, the Ambassade is truly comfortable and, not surprisingly, often full. Rambling through ten handsome merchant's houses, it blends good antiques with excellent modern service. Popular with writers, the library has signed copies of their work. ✆ *Herengracht 341, 1016 AZ • Map L4 • 020 555 0222 • www.ambassade-hotel.nl • €€€*

3 Seven Bridges
A tired bridge-spotter can count seven from this charming hotel. Immaculately decorated, it has wooden floors, Persian carpets and furniture that would grace any auction-house catalogue. There are no public rooms, so you can have breakfast in bed without a twinge of guilt. ✆ *Reguliersgracht 31, 1017 LK • Map E5 • 020 623 1329 • www.seven bridgeshotel.nl • €€*

4 De Filosoof
This unique hotel's love affair with philosophy goes beyond its name; each room is designed in a different philosophical and cultural style. ✆ *Anna van den Vondelstraat 6, 1054 GZ • Map B5 • 020 683 3013 • www.sandton.eu/amsterdam • €€*

5 Amsterdam Wiechmann
Made from three well-kept canal houses, the Wiechmann has been polishing its welcome for more than 50 years. Wooden floors, beams and panelling set off antique furniture and Oriental rugs, and the bedrooms are attractively simple. ✆ *Prinsengracht 328–32, 1016 HX • Map K4 • 020 626 3321 • www.hotelwiechmann.nl • €€*

6 Lloyd Hotel
The city's leading art hotel lies in the heart of the gentrified Eastern Docklands. Uniquely, the 117 rooms rank from one- to five-star and have all been individually created by contemporary Dutch designers. ✆ *Oostelijke Handelskade 34, 1019 BN • 020 561 3636 • www.lloydhotel.com • €€€–€€€€€*

7 Seven One Seven
This is a luxuriously laid-back hotel in a five-star neighbourhood, where beautiful antiques complement the even more beautiful guests. Breakfast, tea and evening drinks are included in the rate. ✆ *Prinsengracht 717, 1017 JW • Map E5 • 020 427 0717 • www. 717hotel.nl • €€€€€*

8 Canal House
This hotel brings Dutch art and history into the 21st century. Original timber beams and ornate ceilings sit comfortably in a contemporary setting inspired by the light and dark of traditional Dutch paintings, and rich fabrics of Dutch traders. The restaurant is good value, with excellent food and a garden view. ✆ *Keizersgracht 148, 1015 CX • Map 2L • 020 673 7223 • www.canalhouse.nl • €€€€*

9 The Toren
This graceful but comfortable 17th-century canal house has all the modern technology you could wish for. Deluxe rooms have a canal view and a Jacuzzi. ✆ *Keizersgracht 164, 1015 CZ • Map L2 • 020 622 6352 • www.thetoren.nl • €€€€€*

10 Agora
Overlooking the Singel and conveniently close to the huge floating flower market, this small, intimate hotel also has a peaceful garden. Wooden beams, good furniture, modern bathrooms and reasonable rates make this place hard for anyone to resist. ✆ *Singel 462, 1017 AW • Map M5 • 020 627 2200 • www.hotelagora.nl • €€*

 Recommend your favourite hotel on traveldk.com

Left **Rembrandt** Right **NH Schiller**

TOP 10 Family Hotels

1 Owl
Although there are no particular facilities for children (beyond triple rooms, babysitting and cots for babies), this family-run hotel in the Museum Quarter is noted for its friendliness. A stuffed owl in an alcove provides the name. Rooms are plain but tastefully decorated and there is a pleasant garden. ✆ *Roemer Visscherstraat 1, 1054 EV • Map C5 • 020 618 9484 • www.owl-hotel.nl • €€*

2 Hotel Arena
This four-star hotel is close to the Tropenmuseum and Artis Royal Zoo (see p123). Younger children will love the location, while teenagers will enjoy the club nights at weekends. Although there is only one family room, extra beds may be requested, and the designer suites are very nice. ✆ *'s Gravesandestraat 51, 1092 AA • Map G5 • 020 850 2400 • www.hotelarena.nl • €€*

3 Singel
Children who love animals will enjoy staying opposite the Poezenboot (see p10). The family-run hotel has an excellent location on a pretty stretch of the Singel, and small but characterful rooms. Under-two-year-olds stay for free. ✆ *Singel 13–17, 1012 VC • Map N1 • 020 626 3108 • www.singelhotel.nl • €€€*

4 Amsterdam House
Treat the children to life aboard a houseboat. Amsterdam House has eight of them available for short or long rentals, as well as apartments and hotel rooms. ✆ *'s-Gravelandseveer 7, 1011 KM • Map N5 • 020 626 2577 • www.amsterdamhouse.com • €€*

5 Estheréa
In the same family for three generations, this elegant hotel mixes modern facilities with traditional surroundings and a warm atmosphere. There are family rooms, some of which overlook the courtyard, and a babysitting service. ✆ *Singel 303, 1012 WJ • Map M4 • 020 624 5146 • www.estherea.nl • €€€€*

6 't Jagershuis
This small waterfront inn is a good option for families who prefer to stay outside the city centre. Just 10 km (6 miles) from the city by bus or bicycle, it's in a charming village (see p128), and there are facilities available for families. ✆ *Amstelzijde 2–4, 1184 VA Ouderkerk aan de Amstel • 020 496 2020 • www.jagershuis.com • Dis. access • €€€*

7 Aadam Wihelmina
This is an excellent two star hotel in the Museum Quarter, with three- and four-bedded rooms. The yellow breakfast room is particularly jolly. ✆ *Koninginneweg 169, 1075 CN • 020 662 5467 • www.hotel-aadam-wilhelmina.nl • €€*

8 Rembrandt
This immaculate, good-value hotel has a wonderful antique breakfast room and spacious contemporary bedrooms that can accommodate up to six people. ✆ *Plantage Middenlaan 17, 1018 DA • Map F4 • 020 627 2714 • www. hotel rembrandt.nl • €*

9 NH Schiller
Teenagers might put up with parents in this famous Art Deco hotel overlooking the neon glare of Rembrandtplein. There are plenty of facilities to keep parents entertained while the kids explore the buzzing nightlife. ✆ *Rembrandtplein 26, 1017 CV • Map N6 • 020 554 0700 • www. nh-hotels.com • Dis. access • €€€€€*

10 Albus Hotel
Parents may prefer old-world character, but children usually like their hotels to look spanking new, like this four-star hotel in the Canal Ring. Some of the rooms sleep up to three or four people, and there is a brasserie for breakfast and snacks. ✆ *Vijzelstraat 49, 1017 HE • Map N6 • 020 530 6200 • www.albushotel.com • Dis. access • €€€*

Note: *Unless otherwise stated, all hotels accept credit cards and have en-suite bathrooms.*

Grand Hotel Amrâth

TOP 10 Business Hotels

1 Qbic Hotel Amsterdam WTC

Its location within Amsterdam's World Trade Centre makes this pod hotel ideal for business travellers. Its no frills, "cheap chic" concept comes in the form of "Cubi", a cube-shaped space with mood lighting and a Hästens bed. ✪ WTC, Mathijs Vermeulenpad 1, 1077 XX • 043 321 1111 • www. qbichotels.com • €€€€

2 Radisson Blu Hotel

Situated around a dramatic atrium, this well-run hotel comprises several old houses, a paper factory and a 19th-century vicarage, part of which is now a lovely candlelit bar. The health and conference centres are across the road, connected by a tunnel. ✪ Rusland 17, 1012 CK • Map N4 • 020 623 1231 • www.radissonblu. com /hotel-amsterdam • Dis. access • €€€€

3 Park Plaza Victoria Amsterdam

On the corner of Damrak and opposite Centraal Station, this monumental building has a surprizingly calm and gracious interior. The hotel has a Business Centre, extensive conference facilities and a health and fitness centre. ✪ Damrak 1–5, 012 LG • Map P1 • 020 623 4255 • www.parkplazaamsterdam .com • Dis. access • €€€€€

4 Renaissance Amsterdam

A range of facilities at reasonable rates distinguishes this central hotel. There are meeting rooms and a business centre, as well as a conference centre in a former 17th-century church. The hotel has comfortable rooms and suites, a gym, brown café, boat dock and car park. ✪ Kattengat 1, 1012 SZ • Map N1 • 020 621 2223 • www.renaissance amsterdamhotel.com • Dis. access • €€€€€

5 Crowne Plaza Amsterdam City Centre

A straightforward city-centre business hotel with good business facilities and a fitness centre, and the bonus of New Dorrius, their excellent restaurant (see p58). ✪ Nieuwezijds Voorburgwal 5, 1012 RC • Map N1 • 020 620 0500 • www. crowneplaza.com • Dis. access • €€€€€

6 Okura

Conveniently situated for the RIA Congresgebou, the Okura offers top-of-the-range luxury and facilities to business travellers. It has four restaurants, a brasserie and two bars including the two-Michelin-Star Ciel Bleu perched on its 23rd floor. ✪ Ferdinand Bolstraat 333, 1072 LH • 020 678 7111 • www.okura.nl • Dis. access • €€€€€

7 Grand Hotel Amrâth

Merging classic Art Nouveau style with five-star modish comforts, facilities include boardrooms and banquet halls with AV equipment and a wellness centre. ✪ Prins Hendrikkade 108, 1011 AK • Map Q2 • 020 552 0000 • www.amrathamsterdam. com • €€€€€

8 DoubleTree by Hilton

This sleek, modern hotel is the biggest in central Amsterdam, with 20 conference halls. Rooms come equipped with iMac computers and free Wi-Fi. The SkyLounge on the 11th floor offers breathtaking harbour views. ✪ Oosterdoksstraat 4, 1011 DK • Map R2 • 020 530 0800 • www. doubletree.hilton.com/ amsterdam • Dis. access • €€€– €€€€€

9 Residence Le Coin

In the University District, this smart complex of studios, each with kitchenette, is popular with visiting academics. ✪ Nieuwe Doelenstraat 5, 1012 CP • Map N5 • 020 524 6800 • www.lecoin.nl • €€

10 Atlas

Friendly and efficient, though with no particular business facilities, this Art Nouveau house is near Vondelpark. ✪ Van Eeghenstraat 64, 1071 GK • Map C6 • 020 676 6336 • www.hotelatlas.nl • €€

Left **Quentin England** Right **Quentin**

🔟 Gay Hotels

1 Quentin England
A row of seven unusual houses in this street represents the architectural styles of seven different nations. This cosy, gay-friendly establishment occupies the English cottage and the Netherlands house next door. ⌖ *Roemer Visscherstraat 30, 1054 EZ • Map C5 • 020 616 6032 • www.quentinhotels.com • Dis. access • €€*

2 Quentin
A prime example of an Amsterdam hotel that, although not exclusively gay, extends a warm welcome to its many gay guests. Women in particular make this friendly, well-kept little hotel near Leidseplein their base, as do visiting musicians – Paradiso and Melkweg are nearby *(see pp54–5)*. ⌖ *Leidsekade 89, 1017 PN • Map J6 • 020 626 2187 • www.quentin hotels.com • €€*

3 Amistad
Exclusively gay, this old hotel has been vamped up. The rooms are stylish, with red being the predominant colour, and some rooms have shared facilities. Self-catering apartments and penthouses are also available. Breakfast is served until 1pm. It is close to gay clubs and saunas. ⌖ *Kerkstraat 42, 1017 GM • Map L6 • 020 624 8074 • www.amistad. nl • €€*

4 Hotel Downtown Amsterdam
In the gay enclave of Kerkstraat, this friendly hotel is in a great location. There are 24 bright and clean rooms, all with en-suite facilities. ⌖ *Kerkstraat 25, 1017 GA • Map L6 • 020 777 6877 • www. hoteldowntown.nl • €€*

5 Golden Bear
This exclusively gay hotel has been popular since it first opened in 1948. With a pretty façade and 11 clean, neat rooms, some with shared facilities, it's situated in Kerkstraat – a street in the Canal Ring where there are several other gay venues. ⌖ *Kerkstraat 37, 1017 GB • Map L6 • 020 624 4785 • www.goldenbear.nl • €€*

6 Waterfront
Bedrooms are a cut above at this smart, gay-friendly hotel within easy reach of the artistic treasures of the Museum Quarter and the historic centre. The distinctive reception room has a black-and-white floor and antique furniture. ⌖ *Singel 458, 1017 AW • Map M5 • 020 421 6621 • www. hotelwaterfront.nl • €€€*

7 Sander
A gay-friendly hotel situated behind the Concertgebouw in the Museum Quarter. Though plain, most of the 20 rooms are spacious, some with features such

as fireplaces and window seats. The breakfast room opens on to a pretty garden. ⌖ *Jacob Obrecht-straat 69 • Map C6 • 020 662 7574 • www.hotel-sander.nl • Dis. access • €€*

8 Amsterdam Hostel Orfeo
While no longer exclusively gay, this hotel has a good location close to Leidseplein. There is also a fun bar that has a great happy hour. ⌖ *Leid-sekruisstraat 14, 1017 RH • Map D5 • 020 623 1347 • www.amsterdamhostel orfeo.com • €*

9 Mauro Mansion
Conveniently located near the Centraal Station, this lovely boutique hotel welcomes gay and straight guests. Owners Berry and Marcel have created a romantic and restful environment. Choose one of the rooms with a canal view. ⌖ *Geldersekade 16, 1012 BH • Map Q2 • 061 297 4594 • www.mauro mansion.com • €€€*

10 Apartments Unlimited
Not a hotel but a service offering a variety of accommodation options in central Amsterdam: choose from several studios, apartments, houseboats and an exclusively gay B&B near Amstel River. ⌖ *020 620 1545 • www.apartments-unlimited.com/cities/ amsterdam • €€*

Note: *Unless otherwise stated, all hotels accept credit cards and have en-suite bathrooms.*

Amstel Botel

TOP 10 Budget Hotels

Hermitage Hotel

Close to the Amstel, on a peaceful canal, the Hermitage Hotel is clean and well organized. The rooms on the top floor have the most character, but all rooms have a shower and a toilet. ◎ *Nieuwe Keizersgracht 16, 1018 DR • Map Q6 • 020 623 8259 • www.hotel hermitageamsterdam.com • €€*

De Munck

Originally built for a ship's captain and within hailing distance of the Amstel, an otherwise traditional interior has been given a dose of 1960s retro. Rooms in the De Munck are airy and clean, and there is a garden. ◎ *Achtergracht 3, 1017 WL • Map E5 • 020 623 6283 • www. hoteldemunck.com • €€*

Amstel Botel

The idea of staying on a boat has a certain charm, but the downside of the Amstel Botel is that it isn't moored in central Amsterdam, and the rooms (or cabins if you prefer) on this floating hotel are small. The upside is getting three-star accommodation at a very reasonable price and good views over the harbour. There is also a ferry that will take you to Centraal Station in 10–15 minutes. ◎ *NDSM Pier 3 (Amsterdam-Noord) • 020 626 4247 • www.amstel botel.com • €€*

Bicycle Hotel Amsterdam

Clean, cheap, simple rooms away from the tourist traps, with bikes for rent, free maps and advice on routes and sights attract a young clientele. What might be a lounge elsewhere is "a chill-out zone" here in De Pijp. ◎ *Van Ostadestraat 123, 1072 SV • 020 679 3452 • www.bicyclehotel. com • €*

Museumzicht

You can peer down into the lovely Rijksmuseum garden from the plain rooms at the back of this modest hotel occupying the top floors of a Victorian house. The Museumzicht's greatest asset is its splendid location. ◎ *Jan Luykenstraat 22, 1071 CN • Map C5 • 020 671 2954 • €*

Acacia

Steep stairs, simple rooms (some with epic canal views) and a pleasant breakfast room are a quarter of an hour's walk away from the city centre, in Jordaan. The charming owners also offer self-catering studios, and a houseboat on a nearby canal. ◎ *Lindengracht 251, 1015 KH • Map C2 • 020 622 1460 • www. hotelacacia.nl • €*

Travel Hotel Amsterdam

Though this hotel is very basic, the location, in the heart of Oude Zijde and next to the Red Light District, makes up for the lack of facilities. There is also a 24-hour bar to keep guests entertained. ◎ *Beursstraat 23, 1012 JV • Map N2 • 020 626 6532 • www.travelhotel.nl • €*

Chic and Basic

Chic and Basic offers a budget solution in an up-market location, right in the western canal ring. This two-star gem is hidden behind four 300-year-old canal houses, is modern and comfortable, with Wi-Fi in every room. ◎ *Herengracht 13–19, 1015 BA • Map M1 • 020 522 2345 • www.chicandbasic.com • Dis. access • €€*

The Winston Hotel

On the doorstep of the Red Light District, this inexpensive art hotel has vibrant rooms, individually designed by local art students. It attracts a young crowd, in part because of the adjacent club, so expect a little noise. ◎ *Warmoesstraat 129, 1012 JA • Map N3 • 020 623 1380 • www. winston.nl • €–€€*

Hegra

Its prime location on the lovely Herengracht, its prices and the warmth of its welcome make up for the (comfortable) rooms being rather on the small side. ◎ *Herengracht 269, 1016 BJ • Map L3 • 020 623 7877 • www. hotelhegra.nl • €*

General Index

Acknowledgements

Main Contributors

Fiona Duncan and Leonie Glass are a British travel-writing team of 15 years standing. They are co-authors of three guides in Duncan Petersen's *3-D City Guides* series, including a guide to Amsterdam; *Paris Walks*, in the *On Foot City Guides* series; and several *Charming Small Hotel* guides.

Additional Contributors

Pip Farquharson (Top 10 Bars, Performing Arts Venues and Clubs; all Around Town listings) is a journalist and long-time inhabitant of Amsterdam. She publishes her own alternative listings guide to the city, www.underwateramsterdam.com.

Rodney Bolt (Top 10 Cafés, Bars and Restaurants) also lives in Amsterdam. He is a novelist (History Play), and author of several travel guides.

Produced by DP Services, a division of DUNCAN PETERSEN PUBLISHING LTD

Project Editor Chris Barstow
Designer Janis Utton
Picture Researcher Lily Sellar
Indexer Hilary Bird
Main Photographer Anthony Souter
Additional Photography Max Alexander, Steve Gorton, Rupert Horrox, Kim Sayer, Neil Setchfield, Clive Streeter, Gerard van Vuuren, Gavin Wollard
Illustrator chrisorr.com
Maps Dominic Beddow, Simonetta Giori (Draughtsman Ltd)

FOR DORLING KINDERSLEY

Publisher Douglas Amrine
Senior Art Editor Marisa Renzullo
Senior Cartographic Editor Casper Morris
DTP Jason Little
Production Sarah Dodd
Picture Librarian Charlotte Oster
Fact Checker Gerard van Vuuren
Additional Design and Editorial Assistance Emma Anacootee, Declan Aylward, Marta Bescos, Simon Davis, Anna Freiberger, Camilla Gersh, Integrated Publishing Solutions, Julia Gorodecky, Priya Kukadia, Carly Madden, Sam Merrell, Daniel Milton, Marianne Petrou, Mindy Ran, Erin Richards, Ellen Root, Sadie Smith

Picture Credits

Works of art have been reproduced with the permission of the following copyright holders: ©ADAGP, Paris and DACS, London 2011 *Portrait of Bernard's Grandmother*, 1887, by Emile Bernard 18b; ©DACS, 2011, *Children with Dog*, 1950, by Karel Appel 47bl; ©Munch Museum/Munch-Ellingsen Group, BONO, Oslo, DACS, London 2011, *Two Women on the Beach*, 1898, by Edvard Munch 14tl.

The publishers would like to thank the following individuals, companies and picture libraries for permission to reproduce their photographs:

AKG LONDON: 38tr, 49rd, *Dutch Battle Ships*, 1863, by Ludolf Backhuysen 27b; Residenzmuseum, Munich, *Peter the Great*, 1717 by Jean Marc Nattier 10c; Kunsthistorisches Museum, Erich Lessing, *Allegory of Painting*, c1665-66, by Jan Vermeer 46tl. AMSTERDAM ARENA: 71rd, 129tr. AMSTERDAM VILLAGE COMPANY: 54bl. AMSTERDAM MUSEUM: 7cla, 24t, 25tc, 25cra, 25bl, 26b, 40b, 107b; *Bird's Eye View of Amsterdam*, 1538, by Cornelis Anthonisz 24c; *The Gouden Leeuw on the Ij at Amsterdam*, 1686, by Willem van de Velde the younger 24b; *The Anatomy Lesson of Dr Jan Deijman*, 1656, by Rembrandt van Rijn 25c; *Dam Square with the New Town Hall under Construction*, 1656, by Johannes Lingelbach 26tl; *Portrait of 17 Guards* by Cornelis Anthonisz 26tr; *Silver Marriage Cup* by Gerrit Valek 27c; *Arrival of Napoleon at Dam Square*, 1811 by Matheus I van Bree 38tl; *Tulp en Spin* by B. Assteijn 83b. ©AFF/AFS AMSTERDAM, THE NETHERLANDS: 7bl, 32tl, 32br, 32-33c, 33cr, 33b, 47br. BAZAR: 61tl. BIJBELS MUSEUM: Ernest Annyas 101br; EDDY BOEUE: 99tl; COBRA MUSEUM VOOR MODERNE KUNST, AMSTELVEEN: ©DACS, 2011, *Children with Dog*, 1950, by Karel Appel 47bl. THE COLLEGE HOTEL: 118tl. COSTER DIAMONDS: 116b, 117tr. DAALDER ETEN & DRINKEN: 60tl. EYE FILM INSTITUTE: 127tl. GEMEENTEARCHIEF: Doriann Kransberg 99b. GETTY IMAGES: 47tr. GO GALLERY: Herman van Heusden 97tl. GRAND HOTEL AMRATH: 147. DE HOLLANDSCHE MANEGE: 119tl. HET BLAUWE THEEHUIS: 50tl. HOTEL DE L'EUROPE: 52tl. HORTUS BOTANICUS:

67bl. JAN DERWIG ARCHITECTUUR FOTOGRAFIE: 126b. JOODS HISTORISCH MUSEUM: Jeroen Nooter 48tl, 48tr, 48b. JORDAAN FESTIVAL: Jan Willem Groen 70br. KONINKLIJK THEATER CARRÉ: Rob Liot 122tl. LEONARDO MEDIABANK: 145tl. MARY EVANS PICTURE LIBRARY: 39br. MULLIGANS: 110tl. MUSEUM AMSTELKRING: Gert Jan van Rooij 20tl, 20br, 21cr, 21cb, 21bl, 82c. MUSEUM HET REMBRANDTHUIS: 41t, 76tr. MUSEUM ONS' LIEVE HEER OP SOLDER: 6br; 20clb; 20-21c. MUSEUM VAN LOON: Maarten Brinkgreve 7cr, 30tl, 30cb, 30cr, 30-31c, 31cr, 31bc; *The Romantic Double Portrait*, 1791, by J.F.A Tischbein 31bl. NEDERLANDS SCHEEPVAARTMUSEUM, AMSTERDAM: 40tr, *Plan of Amsterdam*, 1648, 11b. NEMO SCIENCE AND TECHNOLOGY CENTER: 129bl; NH SCHILLER HOTEL: 113tl; 146tr. OPENBARE BIBLIOTHEEK AMSTERDAM: Annetje van Praag 141tl. PA PHOTOS: 39bl. PATHÉ TUSCHINSKI, AMSTERDAM: 49t, 106cr. DE PEPERWORTEL: 119tr. PICTURE BOX: 64tl, 64b, 70tl, 70tr; Cuypers, Fotografie Igno 42tl; Amerens Hedwich 23tc, 23c, 40tl; Leeden van der Henk 71tl. LOS PILONES: 103tl. RIJKSMUSEUM, AMSTERDAM: 13cr, 13cb, 13bl, 13tr, 14tr; *The Kitchen Maid*, 1658, by Johannes Vermeer 6cl, 12b; *Windmill on the Polder Wate* c.1889, by Paul Joseph Constantin Gabriel 13ca; ©Munch Museum/ Munch-Ellingsen Group, BONO, Oslo, DACS, London 2011, *Two Women on the Beach*, 1898, by Edvard Munch 14tl; *Gallant Conversation*, 1654, by Gerard ter Borch II 14tc; *Self Portrait as St Paul*, 1661, by Rembrandt van Rijn 15c; *Company of Frans Banning Cocq and Willem van Ruytenburch* known as *The Night Watch*, 1642, by Rembrandt van Rijn 15b; *Self Portrait at a Young Age*, 1628, by Rembrandt van Rijn 46c. SKINS COSMETICS LOUNGE: 104tr; STADSSCHOUWBURG: 57tl; SUGAR FACTORY: Atilla Tassy 55tr: SUPPERCLUB: Kim van der Leden (www.photo-kim.com) 86tr; DE TAART VAN M'N TANTE: Peter Sabelis 50tr. TROPENTHEATER: 56tr, 112cr. TULIP MUSEUM: 90tr. VAN GOGH MUSEUM, AMSTERDAM (VINCENT VAN GOGH FOUNDATION): Luuk Kramer 16cl; *View of Prins Hendrikkade* by Claude Monet 18tc; Vincent van Gogh Foundation 19cl; *Vase with Sunflowers*, 1889, by Vincent van Gogh 6cb, 16c; *The Potato Eaters*, 1889 by Vincent van Gogh 16cb; *A Pair of Shoes*, 1885, by Vincent van Gogh 17tr; *Self Portrait as an Artist*, 1887, by Vincent van Gogh 17ca; *Wheatfield with Crows*, 1890, by Vincent van Gogh 17b, 46tr; *Exhausted Maenads after the Dance*, 1875, by L Alma Tadema 18tl; *Self Portrait with a Portrait of Bernard, 'Les Misérables'*, 1888, by Paul Gauguin 18tr; ©ADAGP, Paris and DACS, London 2011 *Portrait of Bernard's Grandmother*, 1887, by Emile Bernard 18b; *The Bedroom at Arles*, 1888, by Vincent van Gogh 19b. WINSTON KINGDOM: 54tl; WORLD OF AJAX: 127b; YELLOW BICYCLE: 136tr. XTRACOLD: 52bl.

All other images © Dorling Kindersley. See www.dkimages.com for more information.

Special Editions of DK Travel Guides

DK Travel Guides can be purchased in bulk quantities at discounted prices for use in promotions or as premiums. We are also able to offer special editions and personalized jackets, corporate imprints, and excerpts from all of our books, tailored specifically to meet your own needs.

To find out more, please contact:
(in the US) **SpecialSales@dk.com**
(in the UK) **TravelSpecialSales@uk.dk.com**
(in Canada) DK Special Sales at **general@tourmaline.ca**
(in Australia) **business.development@pearson.com.au**

Phrase Book

In an Emergency

Help!	**Help!**	Help
Stop!	**Stop!**	Stop
Call a doctor.	**Haal een dokter.**	Haal uhn dok-tur
Call an ambulance.	**Bel een ambulance.**	Bell uhn ahm-bew-luhns-uh
Call the police.	**Roep de politie.**	Roop duh poe-leet-see
Call the fire brigade.	**Roep de brandweer.**	Roop duh brahnt-vheer

Communication Essentials

Yes	**Ja**	Yaa
No	**Nee**	Nay
Please	**Alstublieft**	Ahls-tew-bleeft
Thank you	**Dank u**	Dahnk-ew
Excuse me	**Pardon**	Pahr-don
Hello	**Hallo**	Hallo
Goodbye	**Dag**	Dahgh
Good night	**Goede nacht**	ghoode naht
morning	**Morgen**	Mor-ghuh
afternoon	**Middag**	Mid-dahgh
evening	**Avond**	Ah-vohnd
What?	**Wat?**	Vhat
When?	**Wanneer?**	Vhan-eer
Why?	**Waarom?**	Vhaar-om
Where?	**Waar?**	Vhaar

Useful Phrases

How are you?	**Hoe gaat het ermee?**	Hoo ghaat het er-may
Very well, thank you.	**Heel goed, dank u.**	Hayl ghoot, dahnk ew
How do you do?	**Hoe maakt u het?**	Hoo maakt ew het
That's fine.	**Prima.**	Pree-mah
Where is/are ...?	**Waar is/zijn?**	Vhaar iss/zayn
How do I get to ...?	**Hoe kom ik naar ...?**	Hoo kom ik naar
Do you speak English?	**Spreekt u Engels?**	Spraykt ew eng-uhls
I don't understand.	**Ik snap het niet.**	Ik snahp het neet
I'm sorry.	**Sorry.**	Sorry

Shopping

How much does this cost?	**Hoeveel kost dit?**	Hoo-vayl kost dit?
I would like ...	**Ik wil graag ...**	Ik vhil ghraakh
Do you have ...?	**Heeft u ...?**	Hayft ew
Do you take credit cards?	**Neemt u credit cards aan?**	Naymt ew credit cards aan
Do you take traveller's cheques?	**Neemt u reischeques aan?**	Naymt ew raiys-sheks aan
What time do you open/close?	**Hoe laat gaat u open/dicht?**	Hoo laat ghaat ew opuh/dikht
this one	**deze**	day-zuh
that one	**Die**	dee
expensive	**duur**	dewr
cheap	**goedkoop**	ghoot-koap
size	**maat**	maat
white	**wit**	vhit
black	**zwart**	zvhahrt
red	**rood**	roat
yellow	**geel**	ghayl
green	**groen**	ghroon
blue	**blauw**	blah-ew

Types of Shop

antique shop	**antiekwinkel**	ahn-teek-vhin-kul
bakery	**bakker**	bah-ker
bank	**bank**	bahnk
bookshop	**boekwinkel**	book-vhin-kul
butcher	**slager**	slaakh-er
cake shop	**banketbakkerij**	bahnk-et-bahk-er-aiy
cheese shop	**kaaswinkel**	kaas-vhin-kul
chemist	**apotheek**	ah-poe-taiyk
chip shop	**patatzaak**	pah-taht-zaak
delicatessen	**delicatessen**	daylee-kah-tes-suh
department store	**warenhuis**	vhaar-uh-houws
fishmonger	**viswinkel**	viss-vhin-kul
greengrocer	**groenteboer**	ghroon-tuh-boor
hairdresser	**kapper**	kah-per
market	**markt**	mahrkt
newsagent	**krantenwinkel**	krahn-tuh-vhin-kul
post office	**postkantoor**	pohst-kahn-tor
shoe shop	**schoenenwinkel**	sghoo-nuh-vhin-kul
supermarket	**supermarkt**	sew-per-mahrkt
tobacconist	**sigarenwinkel**	see-ghaa-ruh-vhin-kul
travel agent	**reisburo**	raiys-bew-roa

Sightseeing

art gallery	**galerie**	ghaller-ee
bus station	**busstation**	buhs-stah-shown
bus ticket	**ov chipkaart**	o-vay chip-kaahrt
cathedral	**kathedraal**	kah-tuh-draal
church	**kerk**	kehrk
closed on public holidays	**op feestdagen gesloten**	op fayst-daa-ghuh ghuh-slow-tuh
day return	**dagretour**	dahgh-ruh-tour
garden	**tuin**	touwn
library	**bibliotheek**	bee-bee-yo-tayk
museum	**museum**	mew-zay-uhm
railway station	**station**	stah-shown
return ticket	**retourtje**	ruh-tour-tyuh
single journey	**enkeltje**	eng-kuhl-tyuh
tourist information	**VVV**	fay fay fay
town hall	**stadhuis**	staht-houws
train	**trein**	tr_aiyn_

Staying in a Hotel

Do you have a vacant room?	**Zijn er nog kamers vrij?**	Zaiyn er nokh kaamers vray
double room	**een twee persoonskamer**	uhn tvhay-per soans-kaa-mer
with double bed	**met een twee persoonsbed**	met uhn tvhay-per-soans beht
twin room	**een kamer met een lits-jumeaux**	uhn kaa-mer met uhn lee-zjoo-moh
single room	**eenpersoons-kamer**	ayn-per-soans-kaa-mer
room with bath	**kamer met bad**	kaa-met baht
shower	**douche**	doosh
porter	**kruier**	krouw-yuh
I have a reservation.	**Ik heb gereseveerd.**	Ik hehp ghuh-ray-sehr-veert

Eating Out

Have you got a table?	**Is er een tafel vrij?**	Iss ehr uhn tah-fuhl vraiy
I'd like to reserve a table.	**Ik wil een tafel reserveren.**	Ik vhil uhn tah-fuhl ray-sehr-veer-uh
breakfast	**het ontbijt**	het ont-baiyt
lunch	**de lunch**	duh lernsh
dinner	**het diner**	het dee-nay
The bill, please.	**Mag ik afrekenen.**	Mukh ik ahf-ray-kuh-nuh
waitress	**serveerster**	sehr-veer-ster
waiter	**meneer**	
menu	**de kaart**	duh kaahrt
starter, first course	**het voorgerecht**	het vohr-ghuh-rekht
main course	**het hoofdgerecht**	het hoaft-ghuh-rekht
dessert	**het nagerecht**	het naa-ghuh-rekht
cover charge	**het couvert**	het koo-vehr
wine list	**de wijnkaart**	duh vhaiyn-kaart
glass	**het glas**	het ghlahss
bottle	**de fles**	duh fless
knife	**het mes**	het mess
fork	**de vork**	duh fork
spoon	**de lepel**	duh lay-pul

Menu Decoder

aardappels	aard-uppuhls	potatoes
azijn	aah-zaiyn	vinegar
biefstuk	beef-stuhk	steak
bier, pils	beer, pilss	beer
boter	boater	butter
brood	broat	bread
cake, taart, gebak	'cake', taahrt, ghuh-bahk	cake, pastry
chocolade	show-coa-laa	chocolate
citroen	see-troon	lemon
cocktail	cocktail	cocktail
droog	droakh	dry
eend	aynt	duck
ei	aiy	egg
garnalen	ghahr-naah-luh	prawns
gebakken	ghuh-bah-ken	fried
gegrild	ghuh-ghrillt	grilled
gekookt	ghuh-koakt	boiled
gepocheerd	ghuh-posh-eert	poached
groenten	ghroon-tuh	vegetables
ham	hahm	ham
haring	haa-ring	herring
hutspot	huht-spot	hot pot
ijs	aiyss	ice, ice cream
jenever	yuh-nay-vhur	gin
kaas	kaas	cheese
kabeljauw	kah-buhl-youw	cod
kip	kip	chicken
koffie	coffee	coffee
kool, rode of witte	coal, roe-duh off vhit-uh	cabbage, red or white
kroket	crow-ket	ragout in bread-crumbs
lamsvlees	lahms-flayss	lamb
mineraalwater	meener-aahl-vhaater	mineral water
mosterd	moss-tehrt	mustard
olie	oh-lee	oil
pannekoek	pah-nuh-kook	pancake
patat frites	pah-taht freet	chips
peper	pay-per	pepper
poffertjes	poffer-tyuhs	tiny buckwheat pancakes
rijst	raiyst	rice

rijsttafel	raiys-tah-ful	Indonesian meal
rode wijn	roe-duh vhaiyn	red wine
rookworst	roak-vhorst	smoked sausage
rundvlees	ruhnt-flayss	beef
saus	souwss	sauce
schaaldieren	skaahl-deeh-ruh	shellfish
scherp	skehrp	hot (spicy)
schol	sghol	plaice
soep	soup	soup
stamppot	stahm-pot	sausage stew
suiker	souw-ker	sugar
thee	tay	tea
tosti	toss-tee	cheese on toast
uien	ouw-yuh	onions
uitsmijter	ouht-smaiy-ter	fried egg on bread with ham
varkensvlees	vahr-kuhns-flayss	pork
vers fruit	fehrss frouwt	fresh fruit
verse jus	vehr-suh zjhew	fresh orange juice
vis	fiss	fish/seafood
vlees	flayss	meat
water	vhaa-ter	water
witte wijn	vhih-tuh vhaiyn	white wine
worst	vhorst	sausage
zout	zouwt	salt

Numbers

1	**een**	ayn
2	**twee**	tvhay
3	**drie**	dree
4	**vier**	feer
5	**vijf**	faiyf
6	**zes**	zess
7	**zeven**	zay-vuh
8	**acht**	ahkht
9	**negen**	nay-guh
10	**tien**	teen
11	**elf**	elf
12	**twaalf**	tvhaalf
13	**dertien**	dehr-teen
14	**veertien**	feer-teen
15	**vijftien**	faiyf-teen
16	**zestien**	zess-teen
17	**zeventien**	zayvuh-teen
18	**achttien**	ahkh-teen
19	**negentien**	nay-ghuh-teen
20	**twintig**	tvhin-tukh
21	**eenentwintig**	aynuh-tvhin-tukh
30	**dertig**	dehr-tukh
40	**veertig**	feer-tukh
50	**vijftig**	faiyf-tukh
60	**zestig**	zess-tukh
70	**zeventig**	zay-vuh-tukh
80	**tachtig**	tahkh-tukh
90	**negentig**	nayguh-tukh
100	**honderd**	hohn-durt
1000	**duizend**	douw-zuhnt
1,000,000	**miljoen**	mill-yoon

Time

one minute	**een minuut**	uhn meen-ewt
one hour	**een uur**	uhn ewr
a day	**een dag**	uhn dahgh
Monday	**maandag**	maan-dahgh
Tuesday	**dinsdag**	dins-dahgh
Wednesday	**woensdag**	vhoons-dahgh
Thursday	**donderdag**	donder-dahgh
Friday	**vrijdag**	vraiy-dahgh
Saturday	**zaterdag**	zaater-dahgh
Sunday	**zondag**	zon-dahgh

Selected Street Index

Selected Street Index